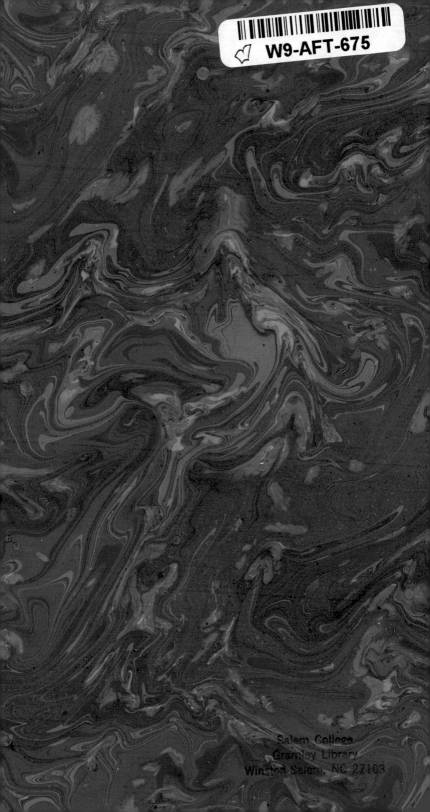

A Word
or Two
Before
You Go....

Also by Jacques Barzun

The House of Intellect
On Writing, Editing, and Publishing
Critical Questions
Simple & Direct
Clio and the Doctors

Jacques Barzun

A Word or Two Before You Go....

 Wesleyan University Press
Middletown, Connecticut

Copyright © 1986 by Jacques Barzun
All rights reserved.

Library of Congress Cataloging-in-Publication Data

Barzun, Jacques, 1907–
A word or two before you go— .

Bibliography: p.
Includes index.
I. English language—Errors of usage.   I. Title.
II. Title: Word or 2 before you go.
PE1460.B378   1986   428   86–22457
ISBN 0–8195–5174–0 (alk. paper)

All inquiries and permissions requests should be addressed to the Publisher, Wesleyan University Press, 110 Mt. Vernon Street, Middletown, Connecticut 06457.

Distributed by Harper & Row Publishers, Keystone Industrial Park, Scranton, Pennsylvania 18512.

Manufactured in the United States of America
First Edition

. . . a word or two before you go:
. . . .
No more of *that*, I pray you, in your letters

Othello, Act V, Sc. 2, ll. 338, 340

PUBLISHER'S NOTE

All but six of the essays in this book appeared in periodicals, some dating as far back as the 1940s, when the criticism of current speech and writing was far from being the popular sport it has become in the last ten years. But despite the recent flurry, the problems Mr. Barzun dealt with remain and his witty admonishing is as fresh as when first published. Mr. Barzun has agreed to allow the reissue of the earlier pieces, although at first reluctant; at our request he searched through files for essays not yet published in a book and undertook to do some revising so that this book could have a balanced view of the subject. Besides the usual, purely verbal, changes, he has removed repetitions and allusions no longer topical. In some cases he drew on several texts to make a single more complete statement. It was the series "On Language" published this year in *Columbia* magazine that prompted the publisher to initiate this book. Appreciative readers of those columns will find them here, modified only to avoid the repetition of examples.

—Wesleyan University Press

CONTENTS

x A Word or Two Before You Go . . . .

PREFACE

Everybody would agree that it takes only a speck of soot in the eye to blot out the sun's glory or the beauty's face. But some people, forgetting it, will argue that to make a fuss about small points of usage is trivial, unworthy of a mind that can deal with high matters.

The fact is that great ideas and deep feelings cannot be fully known or enjoyed, rightly valued or reported, unless they are closely scanned in the only way open to us—matching the experience with the right words. Truth does not easily survive the presence of specks.

Now in a medium as complex as language, accuracy depends on so many details that the best way to achieve it is to make a habit of fussing about every small point, even though neglecting some might occasionally get by. Only by steady care can one keep one's utterance from annoying those who see at once the difference between what is said and what is meant.

This collection of short essays attempts to deal with a variety of such points. All of them were suggested by habits and practices characteristic of current writing. The cultural tendencies thus revealed are what justifies a more than technical treatment aimed solely at better teaching and editing. Language, as Wordsworth said, is not the garment but the incarnation of our thoughts.

A Word or Two Before You Go....

Introductory:
What Are Mistakes and Why

No doubt about it, the meaning of the word literate has taken a hitch upward. It used to designate those who could read and write. Now reviewers praise an author or a book for being literate, as if it were hardly to be expected. This shift is due to the prevalence of bad prose and to a new worry about the state of the language. The term degeneracy has been applied to it, which is not a cheerful thought. But the concern is encouraging. Not long ago it was considered bad manners to criticize speech or writing at any time, even in school, where "self-expression" justified every sort of violence to good sense and good usage. Now there is a many-sided effort to improve writing, on its own ground, like the amateur's stance and swing in golf or tennis.

But while colleges spend large sums on "remedial English" and set up Deans of Writing; and scientific journals hire rewrite staffs for the sake of readable reports; and the press quotes and jokes about government gobbledygook, people continue to talk and think in the same jargon as before. Indeed, they produce and parrot all sorts of questionable speechways. Those same persons give up smoking to avoid cancer, diet to grow more shapely, work on their bad posture or memory, take courses to better their minds or increase their charm, but it never occurs to them to overhaul their vocabulary and grammar, let alone improve the quality of the sounds they utter. Words are so close to thought and to self that changes seem uncalled for or impossible—impossible, that is, from

3

within. It is always easy to pick up the latest catchphrase or the new, distorted meaning of an old word.

Obviously, there is a link between the bad writing now being attacked and our unexamined habits of speech. This relation holds, not because people write exactly as they talk, but because the same deep feelings accompany both forms of expression. The hidden bond is the reason why much of the remedial teaching, much of the editing by publishers of books and journals, and all of the random carping and cursing bring about no improvement.

Two of the causes of decline in *all* modern European languages have been: the doctrines of linguistic "science" and the example of "experimental" art. They come together on the principle of Anything Goes—not in so many words, usually, but in unmistakable effect. Modern grammarians have thundered against rules and fought the idea of correctness. Everybody, they said, has "a right to his or her own ways of speech," unspoiled by criticism; it is snobbish and humiliating to correct. Language lives by alteration—there is no better or worse. What is right now was wrong 200 years ago, so let each of us be as "wrong" as we like now; it will all come out in the wash of Time.

This wisdom was admirably summed up in 1964 by a distinguished linguist, Mr. Allen Walker Read, in the question: "Can a Native Speaker Make Mistakes?" The answer *No* amounted to a law. It disposed at a stroke of all the "Deans of Writing" and all the teachers from kindergarten up. But Mr. Read was not more rash or cynical than his fellow linguists; he was only more honest and forthright.

From the opposite quarter the "right" to manhandle the mother tongue has been justified under another unwritten law—the freedom to experiment (meaning try out), which artists have invoked for two centuries against the critics and the philistines. The result has been poetry and prose, good and bad, that have inspired imitation, conscious or unconscious, in everybody. Novelists and playwrights, manufacturers and advertisers have popularized the various species of poetic distortion. Pulling words about, straining or ignoring their sense, has become a democratic sport, seconded, often, by the need to name new objects and the fun of renaming old ones more "scientifically."

But is not the sovereign people free to play with words and enjoy the fun of watching others do so? And has this license not always existed—twisting, shortening, combining vocables to squeeze new and lively meanings out of familiar sounds—thereby enriching, not destroying, the language? Yes, indeed, word play is a delightful pastime and no sensible being wants to stop it. But since it is a game, it has rules, even if unwritten. One of them is that it should enliven the social hour spontaneously and just for the moment. When someone—Disraeli, perhaps—thought of the failing that makes old people repeat their anecdotes and coined the word *anecdotage*, he deserved a cheer. It was clever—*once*. But neither he nor any thoughtful person wanted to force it into the regular vocabulary. Any joke that turns up everywhere is soon stale—as this very coinage implies.

Again, creators of nonsense—Lewis Carroll, Edward Lear—used their inventive powers in pieces of literature that yielded the humor of nonsense. As such, it was subject to three tests: has it literary quality? is it humorous? is it good nonsense? The third test shows at once how inappropriate playful inventions are for workaday use, and the other two impose a severe standard. Take a recent one, a so-called "portmanteau," which the fat dictionary *International English Usage* lists as an American word: *palimony*. Who made it up is not known; it occurred to somebody while talking or writing about a claim to alimony arising from the break-up of an unmarried couple. Is it on a par with Disraeli's word or any of Lewis Carroll's? Surely not: it can pass as good in the warm flow of conversation, but it lacks style, it is not accurate enough—the pair were not pals, but lovers—and while the humor is weak, the literary charm is nil. Yet the modern mind is ready to turn such words, possibly apt on the spur of the moment, into permanent recruits.

Most of those in vogue are not even as well born as *palimony*. Some attempt a compression too great for deciphering. For example, a would-be school reformer who wants to make pupils *conscious* of the evils of the capitalist system and have them develop a social *conscience* has felt the need to coin *conscientization*—it tells you at once what he means, does it not? And so easy to pronounce, too. Again, an academic philosopher credited with interesting ideas in his own field yielded to a sudden desire for *humbition*, to describe someone whose ambition is legitimate because humble. The word evokes only pity for a good mind o'erthrown.

Even more often, these inventions share the fault of ignoring the really working part of the words drawn on. In *workaholic*, for instance, what is —*holic*? Nothing: —*cohol* is the minimum unit of sense. And so it goes. In one national magazine, *advertorials* are frequent—ads masquerading as news stories. Here again, the telling part *ed* is left out, just as in *reprography* and *infotainment* it is *produc* and *form* that would carry meaning.

The loss of sense can be still more complete: we have had *breathalyzer*, vaguely tied to *analyze*. Now a device exists that turns off the ignition when a driver's breath is suspect; it is dubbed *soberlizer*. No trace of derived meaning remains, not even the *y*. The same void of thought is of course evident in all the —*thon* and —*tron* compounds, of which we are so fond. If we were really as clever as we suppose, we would coin true novelties, as Eastman did with *kodak* and Van Helmont with *gas*. But our imagination seems limited. New York City has adopted *TriBeCa* (the triangle below Canal Street) without a murmur; the city fathers have succumbed to baby talk.

The continual influence of bad examples from without— not limited to new-coined terms—and the natural recourse to what seems like one's own store of words and phrases impose on the writer who wants to be clear the permanent duty of sanitation. He or she must increasingly sort out and clean up what comes in by eye and ear, and reject most of it. This task requires not so much an effort of thought as a scrutiny of feeling: one must detect and repress the wish to be coy, arch, playful, jocular, folksy, learned, mysterious, elegant, and (above all) inventive. These affectations underlie most of the expressions that first present themselves as one begins to write. The emotional colorings do not always appear clearly to the conscious mind, or the words would be dismissed out of hand; rather, they are whispered temptations. The struggle against them is to become master of one's vocabulary instead of mastered by the world's.

For the language that prevails now among people who are serious, schooled, and carrying on the world's work is not made up of "mistakes" here and there. It is *as a whole* more bad than good, inherently clumsy and ponderous: words misunderstood and misapplied, idioms distorted, prepositions used at random, jargon and imagery blanketing thought, novelties multiplying without need, grammar and syntax defied to no purpose. These types of disorder may not as yet warrant the name degeneracy, but they are signs that the spirit and sense of the language, the instinctive *Sprachgefühl*, is at low ebb. It is as if the memory of "how words go" had been totally undone by the tacit "anything goes."

Sometimes, when the general loosening is acknowledged, the excuse is put forward that one must never overlook the merit of the colloquial. After all, what is spoken at work or at play, though rarely exact, is almost always understood. It uses shortcuts, including slang, whose vigor and fecundity have been praised since Mencken's *American Language*. Besides, if we are to speak of feelings, nobody can deny how good natured and democratic the common vocabulary is. Therefore, don't pick it over, killing spontaneity and going precious. Stick to "colorful language" and "racy speech." The past of American English shows what treasures have come from these sources;

our prose tradition from Lincoln and Mark Twain to William James and Hemingway has justified the advice: "Write pretty much as you would speak."

Alas, the benefit of that teaching has long since been garnered. No one has deliberately "written stuffy" for a good while. And the advice has lost its point for another reason, implicit in the description of our current ways: common speech, the colloquial, what one hears all around is *not* racy and colorful; it is dull, heavy, pedantic, choked with pseudo-technical words and roundabout expressions. Some speakers and writers try to add color by steadily using obscene modifiers, but the ordinary tone is the pretentious. We do not know it, but we have fallen back into the worst habits of the eighteenth century: pomposity—different, to be sure—and a conventional set of "(ig)noble" words. Both styles reflect the urge to dress up plain things and simple ideas in something fancy and plush.

So let us cut the cackle about the wonders of the colloquial. Slang is always at hand and everybody draws on it more or less, but is it always so expressive, or is it used merely as a sign of status within a clique? In any case, slang is not everywhere the same and it ages very fast. That alone is enough to make it unsuitable for writing. And then, too, the terms are indefinite or contradictory; their sense depends on tone, glance, or eyebrow. For example, *funky*, as defined by an expert, means: "very good or beautiful; solid; cheap, smelly; or generally, no good."

Far from injecting vigor into the upper layers of speech, the slang of today has managed to destroy or make doubtful more good words than it could make up for in a long time. Whole series—from earlier *fairy* and *pansy* down to *queer*, *faggot*, *adult*, and *gay*—have done nothing but rob the language of irreplaceable resources. Others, such as *ball*, *bomb*, *blow*, *screw* have been left uncertain in slang and unexpectably embarrassing elsewhere. Nowadays, slang rather preys on the straight vocabulary than feeds it new blood; and the loss is made worse by the general abandonment on the part of the educated of *propriety* in every sense of the term. In many ways, more sterling speech (including profanity) is heard among the hard hats at a building site than in a faculty meeting.

Why this inversion of roles? It is due to fear and laziness, principally fear of not being of the crowd and of "one's own time." In writing, the effort to be friendly and informal seduces one into being chummy and slovenly. Writers suppose that their unbuttoned state will lure and coax the reader along. But the reader is not so easily won; he remains free and may not be "conciliated" (as if the situation were adversary) by a folksiness that is obvious pretense. Yet this pretense is found in most of the books that profess to advise and inform, just as verbal promiscuity, the language of the gutter, infects the stage and a large part of fiction. In the former genre, the message seems to be: "Though I know more than you—or how could I presume to inform?—don't think I feel superior. Let my jocular tone suggest my ever-friendly, grinning face." In the latter genre, the boast is: "I have been around and seen the worst: take the nature of reality from me. My free use of what shocks and disgusts shows that I am well qualified to dispel your bourgeois illusions."

Both ploys—for that is all they are—are at bottom condescension and insincerity. To placate without reason someone who wants to inform himself, or to disgust, again without reason, routinely, someone who is as aware of reality as any literary bloke is a gratuitous affront. The writer's real feelings, it must never be forgotten, impart themselves through tone and diction as much as through surface meanings. Writers who want to be known for their plain, straightforward English, their hard-hitting vernacular prose, must be simple and direct in their emotions too.

Guidelines

The Positive Side of Negatives

People for whom words are vivid, tangible things and who are thus intent on meanings, their own and others', tend to be endlessly critical, of themselves and others. They do not like this usage or that phrase, they won't have *contact* as a verb (Rex Stout), they insist that *disinterested* does not mean *uninterested* (Evelyn Waugh), they regard the decline of *cohort* from a band of three hundred to a single *companion* as deplorable: such items of speech are only the first few of a long list of reprovables. Nothing seems to please these people except their own wall-to-wall carping.

This habit of mind earns them sour glances (why so superior?) or at best an attitude of tolerant pity—they can't help nagging, poor things; God made them dissatisfied, and like the crankiness of the sick, one must put up with it.

Of course, the population at large acts in the same way, though about different things, and it is not marked down for its dissatisfactions. Those who perpetually grumble about the government, who curse "the politicians," who find nothing but evil in big business, who condemn indiscriminately capitalism, divorce, technology, Western Europe, the young, the doctors, the lawyers, and the professors—all these critics are licensed by public opinion to vent their displeasure ad lib; they even get credit for being astute and—high praise—irreverent. One further distinction such critics often have: they know less about what they criticize than the word mongers know about words, the reason being that the former do not love politics, business, or the law, as the latter love language.

But let us wipe the slate clean on both sides and make a more profitable point by detailing some positive acts that would satisfy the naggers about words and shut them up forever. Three clear-cut purposes steadily aimed at would do the trick: Economy, Courtesy, and Accuracy.

Economy means making the best use of the words already in the bank, the words everybody knows and understands. If, for example, the exploration of space begins to call for rules and decisions about national and individual rights, call the rules and decisions *space law*. With this currency at hand no need to borrow from Latin or Greek, as a pioneer thinker on the subject has felt compelled to do by coining *astrolaw*.

An interesting fact about linguistic economy as here defined is that, like its counterpart in handling money, it enriches. Every new application or combination of old words to yield a new meaning is akin to extracting ore from mineral deposits; it adds from our own stores instead of importing. We pay heavily for imports such as *astrolaw*. They lack quick intelligibility, harmony with the rest of the vocabulary, and elegance of form. And often, as in this case, they wake distracting echoes—is spatial *astrolaw* somehow related to nautical *astrolabe*?

Courtesy, obviously, is a by-product of the striving for Economy, but that second desirable end must also be sought by itself. It consists in keeping the reader and listener always in mind. They come first; they are our guests, and hence to be well treated. For nobody on earth has taken a pledge to read or listen to us. It therefore behooves us to make the encounter comfortable, indeed pleasant, as we would certainly try to do if it were a matter of entertaining acquaintances at home.

Courtesy is made up of tact and foresight. Tact is literally *touch*. The considerate writer looks for modes of expression that establish and maintain touch with his unknown reader. Can this be done by taking one's favorite short cut to composition and making use of a term or an idea pages ahead of its explanation? by assuming a general understanding of what is in fact one's specialty, with its vocabulary, allusions, and ways of thought? Hardly. But today nearly everyone is a specialist, which means that everyone is also a layman confronting ten thousand surrounding specialties. That situation is what makes tact imperative. Each specialist as writer must foresee and forestall every failure of "touch" with the reader.

Consider the installation of a telephone-answering machine. The booklet of instructions is beautifully printed and here and there well-written. But at the outset the purchaser is asked to make sure of the power supply by the coming on of the LED lights. These are not marked as such on the instrument or shown on the diagram. *A* light does come on, but what makes it LED? Twenty-six pages of close print leave the mystery unsolved. I dare say that nowadays every implement more complex than the dustpan and brush comes with a set of directions, and that these contain at least one such puzzle for the user. One ingenious remedy is: spell it out; anything else is discourteous as well as ambiguous or worse. Spelled out, LED turns out to mean "light-emitting diode," so that *LED lights* is both gibberish and redundant.

Again, a by-product of Courtesy will be Accuracy, which is but another aspect of explicitness. Here the difficulty is double: first, to notice when one falls short of being exact; and second, not to fall beyond the goal, into excess simplicity, as if talking to babes. The road to accuracy lies through the forest of synonyms. The name synonym itself is inexact, for no two words mean the same thing. The groups listed in Roget's *Thesaurus* are not made up of identical twins, but of first and second cousins, whose different characters and styles the exact writer will distinguish.

Nor can he write with Roget always open on his lap. He must by extensive reading acquire a whole crowd of "cousins" to summon up as needed. This effort is intended to replace another crowd: the words in vogue that reduce to one term many different ideas; for example *impact*, which stands (inaccurately) for *importance, effect, influence, result, outcome, pressure, consequence, upshot*—to say nothing of *blow, shock, crash,* or *dent*.

If one looks critically at the many hybrids that are coined these days, one will be surprised to find how many are inaccurate despite their seeming technicality. Go back to *astro-law*, in which the Latin *astra* means *stars*. The new type of law is not concerned with stars, or even planets and moons, but with space. Hence the new word is another misnomer. Accuracy, we infer, calls for close seeing and imagining, which gets rid of vague abstractions. Though the men at the Space Center (NASA be blowed!) keep burbling about EVA (extravehicular activity), sensible journalists keep talking about *space walks*, leaving it to the strollers up there to do what they like. Everybody knows it's a wonderful *activity*.

Cobblers of new words, who probably think of themselves as great creators, have as good an opportunity to shine as their ancient predecessors, who gave us out of their experience so vast a treasury of common words and phrases. Many were specialists, in the sense that they plied a trade—sailing, or weaving, or carpentry. But they liked the common English tongue and they had a fine imagination. For example, some carpenter of genius, to designate a piece of wood or a hinge that is not sunk or recessed into another piece, decided that "it stands proud" in relation to that piece. What could say it better? We are not without minds of equal talent today, people who think *with* the language, instead of against it and stuff it with counterfeits. One such positive mind invented *kneeling bus* and deserves a medal. Another type of mind in his place would have soiled the vocabulary with something like *infra-receptor vehicle* (IRV).

Those of us who do not coin either false or sound currency can encourage the true minters by deliberately preferring the sound to the false till it becomes a habit, almost an instinct, of our speaking and writing selves. This too will have a by-product in the form of enjoyment, the savoring of verbal expression, enhanced by the knowledge of what makes it enjoyable. For example, note the grim irony in someone's recent description of the drug traffic as "the informal branch of the pharmaceutical trade": The wit resides in the simple word *informal*. Let us all try to work as deftly as this with the well chosen and well placed word, and there will be no more groaning about the decay of the mother tongue.

"It Makes No Sense"

Everybody who talks or writes has one remarkable gift: a limitless capacity for uttering words without sense, or contrary to their intended sense. No need to go into the many workaday causes—haste, excitement, ignorance, and the like. But one among them is inexcusable, and that is lack of attention, bland indifference, when the conditions of accuracy and the need for it are present; for example, in a public announcement, a set of directions, an ad, and indeed anything in print. The travel agency states: "Our Grand Tour Includes Destination." The letter from the health insurance office requests: "Please sign the form and return with the bone that was fractured." We laugh or frown and say, "How careless!" We ought also to say, "How rude!" for these absurdities show an author completely self-centered, obviously never schooled to regard the convenience of the other party in the transaction.

For a trans-action is what every ordinary use of language is, even "Ouch!" As such, it entails a moral obligation to avoid misleading, puzzling, confusing, shocking, or annoying the recipient. But to spare another's feelings, to keep from imposing a special effort of understanding, takes a previous effort on one's part; and the burden lies on the one who solicits attention. Unfortunately, the work required cannot be closely specified. The idiotic sentence has been set down, any of us potentially the author—then what? Well, look at it, preferably after it has been put aside for a day or two, and ask yourself whether it still conveys that glowing thought, that enticing

promise, that stern demand, that clear explanation which animated your mind at the outset.

This injunction being very general, it must be broken into
separate steps: first, are any words in the statement capable
of two distinct meanings? Ambiguity is a form of non-sense.
A recent news heading reads: "Philadelphia Aims At Illiteracy." The writer no doubt thought of a target such as a deer
or a hare, which can be brought down by aiming at it with a
gun. But in common parlance *aim* (and also *target*) signify
desirable goals. The fund-raising target is something to be
reached, not brought down; and in that sense Philadelphia's
target, illiteracy, was undoubtedly reached before the campaign began. The same kind of thoughtlessness produced the
headline "Grant to Enlarge Child-Abuse Effort."

It is not solely the failure to analyze, as in this Effort, or the
figurative use of words, as in *aim*, that can distract and offend
the reader. When the hijacked plane in Malta was destroyed,
one reporter wrote that the gunman had thrown a grenade into
the cabin and "killed many of its inhabitants." In the context
the misuse of *inhabitants* is not ludicrous; it is for some obscure reason insulting to the dead. One mutters, "Why couldn't
he think of *occupants*?"

Nonsense—and this is the second fault to look for—often
arises from incoherence, that is, mismatching ideas or words,
or allowing a poor fit among them. A chamber-music group
recommends that "Anyone who can borrow, buy, or steal his
or her way into Alice Tully Hall should do so." This brazen
invitation to crime is no doubt workable in two of the three
ways—*buy* and *steal*, but *borrow* won't do. If the explanation
is "borrow money to pay your way in," then "steal your way
in" loses its light play on words. Besides, the echo of the standard phrase "beg, borrow, or steal" is spoiled by the substitution of *buy*: the net effect is a mess.

A faulty sequence of thoughts is of course just as bad. A
writer on fashion maintains that in the past men's dress was

always more comfortable than women's but that now women are adopting the comfortable features. He goes on as follows, punctuation included: "Finally this masculine mode, this looking for comfort, is very modern and corresponds to the way women live now. And as there is no longer this image, this taboo, this concept, 'belonging to men, belonging to women.' " The "finally" relates to nothing that precedes, any more than the second sentence leads to any conclusion. Some link, or more than one, has dropped out and left mere babble.

It may be objected that in reading the quasi advertising prose from which these last two examples are drawn one should not be too demanding. Yet it is the sort of prose that most people read every day and that they are unconsciously most affected by. Other kinds of writing are in fact no more certain to make sense. Take this biographical note in a leading encyclopedia: "Hating cruelty and suffering as he did, he could never have been satisfied by a life entirely in scholarship." Apparently, deans and curriculum committees inflict such tortures on the faculty that this scholar could stand the sight only on a part-time basis.

Besides such a deliberate yet absurd choice of words, there is the absent-minded choice, doubly culpable because it could and should be seen at once for what it is. It occurs most often with clichés or cast-iron idioms that get said or written as by reflex action. A political analyst points to poll figures that differ from earlier ones and writes, "It may be a sea change." What the sea has to do with voting patterns is precisely nil, but Shakespeare's image "suffer a sea change" sounds like an impressive bit to throw in. More earthy, an official statement tells us: "the proof is in the pudding." (Some will recall that with Whittaker Chambers it was in the pumpkin.) Half-remembered proverbs are dangerous to sense and so are vogue phrases, because these are also vague phrases; they have been bent to fit so many uses that they have lost their first dim meaning—until an unforeseen situation brings it back to life. Thus a witness to an alibi in a murder case stated in an affidavit that "there was no way the suspect could have left that week-end." The plain fact, important at law, is that there were any number of ways he could have left—walked, called a cab, been picked up by a helicopter, and so on. What the witness meant was: "I saw him the whole time."

All it takes to avert the commonest cases of verbal void is to stop and think: "It's a whole new world; it will move slot-machine gaming into the 20th century." That mongrel assemblage of clichés refers to the use of computers in casinos. When the last hurricane of the season caused emergency measures to be taken in Alabama, there was "concern that some would refuse to evacuate." (A little knowledge of medical euphemisms would have helped there.) The heading reads: "Dean of the College: Quote Unquote." What on earth . . . ? How can anything be *unquoted*? Very likely, the original term heard over the air was *end quote*. Whatever it was, the unnecessary phrase shows how a foolish usage winds up in nonsense.

A good listener or reader need not be especially attentive, let alone captious, to feel lucky when he or she encounters plain good sense. The impression that nonsense predominates, which Flaubert recorded a hundred years ago, may be mistaken, but it is very strong. Certainly the verbalizing that goes with new conditions in practical life gives little indication that a desire for sense animates our public models and guides. For evidence, take up any government form; the very terms misstate the facts. When the Commonwealth of Massachusetts has occasion to address a physician about his services to the Rehabilitation Commission, he is addressed as "Dear Vendor" and requested to use his "approved name and number" in future communications. A doctor who has long disapproved of his first name—e.g. Theophilus—is thus free not to use it.

The word "free" reminds me, by association, of what I find one of the worst, because the commonest, of recent deviations from sensical usage. I mean the mindless substitution of *have to* for *must*. Formerly, if one said: "What's that noise

in the basement?—it must be a burglar!" the listener understood very well that the *must* signified no more than a strong
surmise. There is no legal or moral compulsion to have bur-
glars in one's basement. To indicate compulsion, one resorted
to the idiom with *have*, which overlapped the use of *must*:
"You *have to* have a vaccination certificate to get a visa." Now
the distinction is blurred and one hears: "You have to be a
smoker to cough so much," which means: "You cannot cough
so much unless you smoke," and not: "I would guess you are
a smoker, since you cough." Here are actual instances of the
confusion. The first is from a recent novel: " 'But you haven't
to forget that,' said Masters." It takes puzzling out to find
here *you mustn't*. The speaker should at least have said "you
have to not forget." The second case is even more serious; it
concerns an international notice of possible defects in a type
of airplane engine: "British Airways . . . were not unaware of
the problem . . . the British Government *had to get* the directives:" The words here italicized state an obligation and imply
that the British did not *go and get* those directives; whereas the
American spokesman meant: the British *must have received*
the warning. A serious failure of sense, what?

Of course, when the reader is puzzled, the nonsense at least
calls attention to itself. More often, the nonsense is as it were
subcutaneous and goes unnoticed: "It's so important to realize
not just the perception but what really goes on in the sub-
ways." Help!

Making sense is "so important," too, that the very phrase
deserves rescue from its regular misuse. Paradoxically, "make
sense" is most often used contrary to sense. For example, X
announces to his family and friends that he is going to cut
Cadillacs in half, add panels in the middle, and sell the length-
ened car to wealthy ostentators. Everybody around cries out
with one voice, "It makes no sense!" The truth is that if the
words had not raised a clear image, did not make perfect sense,
there could be no loud, unanimous objection. When a series of
words *makes no sense*, the sole appropriate remark is, "What

do you mean?" In other words, *make no sense* is not synonymous with *be sensible*, and thus nine times out of ten *makes no sense* makes nonsense.

Nonsense itself is by now equivocal, having acquired through prose and verse the pleasant second meaning of fanciful, topsy-turvy, and amusing. Nonsense is a difficult literary genre that deserves to be cultivated, and its existence confirms the maxim that the only tolerable nonsense is intentional nonsense. Therefore let us end with a fine recent example: "West Point, N.Y. Under the rules of the contest, any concrete canoe that sinks directly to the bottom of Round Pond is not allowed to continue in the race."

English As She's Not Taught

At an educational conference held in Vancouver last summer* leaders of the Canadian school system agreed that from half to three quarters of their students in the first year of college were incompetent in grammar, syntax, and analysis of thought. What was notable in the discussion was that nearly every participant used the English language with uncommon force and precision. Any looseness or jargon heard there came from the three American guests, of whom I was one. Most of our hosts—Canadian teachers, principals, supervisors, and university instructors—had obviously gone through the mill of a classical education; the chairman made a mild pun involving Latin and was rewarded with an immediate laugh. Yet they declared themselves unable to pass on their linguistic accomplishment to the present school generation and they wanted to know why.

In the United States the same complaint and inquiry has been commonplace for some time. You come across it in the papers. You hear parents, school people, editors and publishers, lawyers and ministers, men of science and of business, lamenting the fact that their charges or their offspring or their employees can neither spell nor write "decent English." The deplorers blame the modern progressive school or the comics or television; they feel that in school and outside, something which they call mental discipline is lacking, and they vaguely connect this lack with a supposed decline in morality, an up-

*That is, in 1952. (Ed.)

24

surge of "crisis." Like everything else, bad English is attributed to our bad times, and the past (which came to an end with the speaker's graduation from college) is credited with one more virtue, that of literary elegance.

The facts seem to me different, the causes much more tangled, and the explanation of our linguistic state at once more complex and less vague. For many years now I have been concerned with the craft of writing and kept busy at the invidious task of improving other people's utterance, and I do not see that performance in grammar and syntax has deteriorated. The level is low but it has not fallen. As a reader of history I am steadily reminded that the writing of any language has always been a hit-and-miss affair. Here is Amos Barrett, our chief source on the battles of Concord and Lexington: "It wont long before their was other minit Compneys . . . We marched Down about a mild or a mild half and we see them acomming . . ." and so on. An illiterate New England farmer? Not so, since he could write; he had been taught and in one way represents "the past." The question he poses is, how do people write who are not professionals or accomplished amateurs? The answer is: badly, at all times.

Writing is at the very least a knack, like drawing or being facile on the piano. Because everybody can speak and form letters, we mistakenly suppose that good, plain, simple writing is within everybody's power. Would we say this of good, straightforward, accurate drawing? Would we say it of melodic sense and correct, fluent harmonizing at the keyboard? Surely not. We say these are "gifts." Well, so is writing, even the writing of a bread-and-butter note or a simple public notice; and this last suggests that something has happened within the last hundred years to change the relation of the written word to daily life.

Whether it is the records we have to keep in every business and profession or the ceaseless communicating at a distance which modern transport and industry require, the world's work is now unmanageable, unthinkable, without "literature." Just see how many steps you can take without being confronted with something written or with the necessity of writing something yourself. Having been away for a couple of weeks during the summer, I find a bill from the window washer, who luckily came on a day when the cleaning woman was in the apartment. His scribble below the date reads: "The windows have been cleaned Wed. 12:30 P.M. Your maid was their to veryfey the statement"—perfectly clear and adequate. One can even appreciate the change of tenses as his mind went from the job just finished to the future when I would be reading this message from the past.

Call this bad writing if you like, it remains perfectly harmless. The danger to the language, if any, does not come from such trifles. It comes rather from the college-bred millions who regularly write and who in the course of their daily work produce the prevailing mixture of jargon, cant, vogue words, and loose imagery that passes for prose. And the greater part of this verbiage is published, circulated, presumably read. A committee won't sit if its drivelings are not destined for print. Even an interoffice memo goes out in sixteen copies and the schoolchildren's compositions appear verbatim in a mimeographed magazine. Multiply these cultural facts by the huge number of activities which (it would seem) exist only to bombard us with paper, and you have found the source of the belief in a "decline" in writing ability—no decline in talent, simply the infinite duplication of dufferism. This it is which leads us into false comparisons and gloomy thoughts.

The rapid deterioration of language is a general phenomenon which is denounced throughout Western Europe. One had only to read the Catalogue of the British Exhibition of 1951 to see the common symptoms in England. Sir Ernest Gowers's excellent little book of a few years earlier, *Plain Words*, was an attempt to cure the universal disease in one congested spot, the Civil Service, which is presumably the most highly educated professional group in Britain.

In France, the newspapers, the reports of Parliamentary debates, and the literary reviews show to what extent ignorance of forms and insensitivity to usage can successfully compete against a training obsessively aimed at verbal competence. And by way of confirmation, M. Jean Delorme, a native observer of the language in French Canada, recently declared the classic speech "infected" on this side of the Atlantic too. As for Germany, a foreign colleague and correspondent of mine, a person of catholic tastes and broad judgment, volunteers the opinion that "people who cultivate good pure German are nowadays generally unpopular, especially among the devotees of newspaper fiction and articles. The universal barbarism of language has already gone well into the grotesque."

So much for the democratic reality. But great as has been the effect of enlarged "literacy," it does not alone account for what is now seen as linguistic decadence. The educated, in fact the leaders of modern thought, have done as much if not more to confuse the judgment. For what is meant by the misnomer "pure speech" is simply a habit of respect toward usage, which ensures a certain fixity in vocabulary, forms, and syntax. Language cannot stand still, but it can change more or less rapidly and violently. During the last hundred years, nearly every intellectual force has worked, in all innocence, against language. We can gauge the result from the disappearance of the dictionary properly so called. Consult one of the best of them, *Webster's New World Dictionary*, and what you find is a miniature encylopedia filled with the explanation of initials, proper names, and entries like "macrosporangium" and "ab-henry," which are not and never will be words of the English language.

The power of words over nature, which has played such a role in human history, is now an exploded belief, a dead emotion. Far from words controlling things, it is now things that dictate words. As soon as science was able to chop up the physical world and recombine it in new forms, language followed suit; and this not only among scientists making up new vocables, but among the people at large, including the supposed guardians of the language.

This helps to explain why the predominant fault of the bad English encountered today is not the crude vulgarism of the untaught but the blithe irresponsibility of the taught. The language is no longer regarded as a common treasure to be kept safe as far as possible. Rather, it is loot from the enemy to be played with, squandered, plastered on for one's adornment. Literary words imperfectly grasped, meanings assumed from bare inspection, monsters spawned for a trivial cause—these are but a few of the signs of squandering. To give examples: the hotel clerk assigning me a room feels bound to mention the well-known person whom "we last hospitalized in that room." Not to lag behind Joyce, the advertiser bids you "slip your feet into these easy-going *leisuals* and breathe a sigh of real comfort."

Undoubtedly these strange desires are often born of the need to ram an idea down unwilling throats. We all fear our neighbor's wandering attention and try to keep him awake by little shocks of singularity or an overdose of meaning. Unfortunately, novelty-hunting proceeds from the known to the unknown by a leap of faith. "It was pleasant," writes the author of very workmanlike detective stories, "to watch her face and find his resentment *vitiate* as he made excuses for her."

It is all very well to say, as one expert has confidently done, that "what certain words really mean is moving toward what they seem to mean," the implication being that after a while everything will be in place. Actually, this leaves meaning nowhere, if only because we are not all moving in step. *The New Yorker* spotted a movie theater sign on which "adultery" was used to mean "adulthood." From an English periodical I learn that some new houses "*affront* the opposite side of the street."

There is no getting around it: meaning implies convention, and the discovery that meanings change does not alter the fact that when convention is broken misunderstanding and chaos are close at hand. Winston Churchill has recounted how Allied leaders nearly came to blows because of the single word *table*, a verb which to the Americans meant dismiss from the discussion, whereas to the English, on the contrary, it meant put on the agenda. This is an extraordinary instance, and the vagaries of those who pervert good words to careless misuse may be thought more often ludicrous than harmful. This would be true if language could digest anything and dispose of it in time. But language is not a kind of giant ostrich. Every defect in the language is a defect in somebody.

For self-protection, no doubt, the contemporary mind is opposed to all this quibbling. It speaks with the backing of popular approval when it says: "Stop it! You understand perfectly well what all these people mean. Don't be a nosy purist looking under the surface and meddling with self-expression." To haggle over language *is* quibbling, of course. All precision is quibbling, whether about decimals in mathematics or grains of drugs in prescriptions. The question is whether in language the results justify the quibble. Well, the public is here the best judge, and it is evident that as a consumer of the written word, the public is always complaining that it cannot understand what it is asked to read.

This brings us back to our first difficulty, how to teach the millions the use of their mother tongue *in composition*. We have made the greater part of the population literate in the sense of able to read and write words. But that is not writing. Even those who profess disdain for the literary art and the literary quibbles respond automatically to good writing, which they find unexpectedly easy to read and retain, mysteriously "pleasant" as compared with their neighbors' matted prose.

The linguists themselves pay lip service to "effective" speech, and themselves write good Standard English: they approve the end while forbidding discrimination among the means.

Thousands of people in the United States today also exercise this discrimination; there is amid the garbage a steady supply of good writing, modestly done and published—in newspapers and magazines, in broadcasting, in millions of ads and public notices, in travel booklets, and other printed matter of all kinds. Good writing is good writing wherever it is found. In condemning, too, one must discriminate.

The failure to do so is one cause of the trouble—the strange cultural trait whose origin I have sketched and which makes us at once indifferent to our language, full of complaints about it, and irresponsible about mangling it still more. In these conditions people who write well learn to do so by virtue of a strong desire, developed usually under necessity: their job requires lucidity, precision, brevity. If they write advertising copy they must not only make it fit the space but make the words yield the tone.

Tone—that is the starting point of any teaching in composition. What effect are you producing and by what verbal means? The fewer the words, and the more transparent they are, the easier they will be to understand. The closer the ideas they stand for and the more natural their linkage, the more easily will the meaning be retained. Simple in appearance, this formula is yet extremely difficult to apply, and even more arduous to teach. You can hardly work on more than one pupil at a time and you must be able to observe and enter into his mind. On his part, the discipline calls for a thorough immersion in the medium. He must form the habit of attending to words, constructions, accents, and etymologies in everything he reads or hears—just as the painter unceasingly notes line and color and the musician tones. The would-be writer has a harder task than other artists, because words are entangled with the business of life and he must stand off from it to look at them, hearing their harmonies and discords. It is an endless duty, which at last becomes partly automatic. The ideal writer would mentally recast his own death sentence as he was reading it—if it was a bad sentence.

Now such a discipline cannot be imposed from without, and not everybody needs it in full. But its principle, which suffices for ordinary purposes, should be made clear to every beginner, child or adult. Unfortunately, the school system, even when progressive, makes writing an irrational chore approached in the mood of rebellion. The school does this in two ways: by requiring length and by concentrating on correctness. I know very well that correctness was supposedly given up long ago. The modern teacher does not mention it. But if the teacher marks spelling and grammatical errors and speaks of little else, what is a child to think? He gets a mark with the comment "imaginative" or "not imaginative enough" and most often: "too short," and he is left with no more idea of composition than a cow in a field has of landscape painting. How *does* one judge the right length and get it out of a reluctant brain? Nobody answers, except perhaps with the word "creative," which has brought unmerited gloom to many a cheerful child. Who can be creative on demand, by next Tuesday, and in the requisite amount? In all but a few chatterboxes, mental frostbite is the only result.

Meanwhile the things that are teachable, the ways of translating the flashes of thought into consecutive sentences, are neglected. They have been, most often, neglected in the teachers themselves. How do *they* write or speak, what do *they* read? If they read and write educational literature, as they often must for advancement, are they fit to teach composition? And what of the teachers of other subjects, whose professional jargon also infects their speech, what is their countervailing effect on a child to whom a good English teacher has just imparted a notion of the writer's craft? Suppose the teacher of a course on "family life" has just been reading *Social Casework* and his mind is irradiated with this: "Familial societality is already a settled question biologically, structured in our inherited bodies and physiology, but the answer to those other questions are not yet safely and irrevocably anatomized." Unless this is immediately thrown up like the nux vomica it is, it will contaminate everybody it touches from pupil to public—in fact the whole blooming familial societality.

The cure is harsh and likely to be unpopular, for it must start with self-denial. It can be initiated by the school but it must not stop there. As many of us as possible must work out of our system, first, all the vogue words that almost always mean nothing but temporary vacancy of mind—such words as *basic, major, overall, personal, values, exciting* (everything from a new handbag to a new baby); then all the wormy expressions indicative of bad conscience, false modesty, and genteelism, as in: "Frankly, I don't know too much about it"—a typical formula which tries through candor and whining to minimize ignorance while claiming a kind of merit for it; finally, all the tribal adornments which if cast off might at last disclose the plain man we think we want to be: no *frames of reference, field theories,* or *apperception protocols*; no *texture, prior to,* or *in terms of*; and the least amount of *coördination, dynamics,* and *concepts.*

After the vocabulary has been cleansed, the patient is ready for what our Canadian friends at the Vancouver conference deplored the lack of in the modern undergraduate: analysis of thought. To show what is meant and let criticism begin at home, I choose an example from a New York City report of 1952 entitled "The English Language Arts." It begins: "Because language arts or English is so—" Stop right there! What are language arts?—A perfectly unnecessary phrase of the kind that needlessly tries to "cover" more than the plain, familiar term, and thus inflates "importance." Next, "language arts or English" is nonsense: ever hear of another language? Moreover, "language arts . . . is" doesn't sound like a happy opening for a report by and to English teachers. Let us go on: English is so what? Well, "language arts or English is so intimately connected with all knowledge and all living, it is the subject which most often bursts the dikes separating it from others." What do you mean, language is *connected* with living? And how does English connect with *all* knowledge and *all* living? Is the practical knowledge of the Russian engineer intimately connected with English? Do the amoebas speak English? And if this intimacy does exist, then what are these dikes that separate English from other subjects? Are these subjects not part of "all knowledge" with which English is connected—or rather, of which it too is a part?

Cruel work, but necessary if anything akin to thought is to arise from the written word. The Neanderthal glimmer from which the quoted sentence sprang is irrecoverable but its developed form should run something like this: "English, being a medium of communication, cannot be confined within set limits like other subjects; to the peoples whose speech it is, all theoretical knowledge, and indeed most of life, is inseparable from its use."

And this is so true that it justifies the operation just performed on the specimen of non-thought. For although it is possible to think without words and to communicate by signs, our civilization depends, as I said before, on the written word. Writing is embodied thought, and the thought is clear or muddy, graspable, or fugitive, according to the purity of the medium. Communication means one thought held in common. What could be more practical than to try making that thought unmistakable?

As for the receiver, the reader, his pleasure or grief is in direct proportion to the pains taken by the writer; to which one can add that the taking of pains brings its special pleasure. I do not mean the satisfaction of vanity, for after a bout of careful writing one is too tired to care; I mean the new perceptions—sensuous or intellectual or comic—to be had all day long in one's encounters with language. Imagine the fun people miss who find nothing remarkable in the sentence (from Sax Rohmer): "The woman's emotions were too tropical for analysis"; or who, trusting too far the wise disallowance of *contact* as a verb, miss the chance of using it on the hottest, stickiest time of year: "On a day like this, I wouldn't contact anybody for the world."

Enigma Variations

Among the classics treasured by those who love words is a little book by Pedro Carolino entitled *New Guide of the Conversation in Portuguese and English*. The work first appeared in the United States in 1883 with an introduction by Mark Twain, who said of it: "whatsoever is perfect in its kind, in literature, is imperishable: nobody can add to the absurdity of this book . . . its immortality is secure."

Certainly the *New Guide* possesses one of the merits of true belles-lettres: it is entirely useless. It would defy the most fanatical utilitarian to make it serve his purpose. Consider the climax of Dialogue 8, "*With the tailor*:—Button me.—It pinches me too much upon the stomach.—That a coat go too well, it must that he be just.—The sleeves have not them great deal wideness?—No, sir, they are well.—Where is the remains from the cloth? It is anything from rest."

Although you must admire the poetic compression and rhetorical subtlety of that dramatic interchange, you may say the subject is too low to permit a judgment on the moral value of Carolino's work. Yet the moral question has to be raised, because since the very time of Carolino's vogue, the eighties and nineties, it has been held that morals make for bad art and all art should be useless.

So let us follow our Portuguese guide into the moral realm: —"Have you heard that we shall have the war?—I have not unterstook to speak of it.—They speak however of a siege.— It was spoken, but it is not true: on contrary, they speak of the peace.—Do you think that you shall have it?—I think yes.

—What is said in town?—It is spoken from a voyage.—When they believe that the king shall start?—It is not know.—Where they tell that he go to?—Some ones tell to Flanders, others in Germany."

Some critics, after this, will judge harshly our misunderstood artist's capacity for coherence. But I maintain that his sensibility is fine though flitting. I should say it is flitting because it is fine. What it yields for our delight is the kaleidoscope of existence. He is a skeptic and asks many questions. He is an existentialist and gives brave arbitrary answers. And again, what compression! In a mere forty-three dialogues, each hardly more than a page, we travel (as he would say) the cosmos. We start for to wish the good morning and end—life being but a walking shadow—with Idiotisms and Proverbs, the maxims of a poignant philosophy: "The necessity don't know the low.—He go to four feet . . .—He is bare. . . ,—He not understand the jest . . . ," all of which added together restate the riddle of life: "To do appearance at a bad game."

Such is the test of great art—to start useless and come out facing the ultimate. If we ask what the secret of Carolinian artistry is, we need only point to the device—the *aesthetic*, if you prefer—that our author created, and of which he remains the sole exemplar and master. I mean the submerged speech—*oratio summersa*, also known among hostile critics as "iceberg rhetoric." What I mean is that Carolino's astonishing effects in English are largely due to his straining his Portuguese visions through the sieve of French ("Yes, sir," he tells us, "I attempts to translate of french by portuguese"). This is what generates the forms: "Is it complete this parlour furniture of damask crimson?" and "That pond it seems me many multiplied of fishes." One needs no proof: the sensibility is Portuguese, the sense is French, the triumphant nonsense is English.

But an art of such elevation alters all our judgments of previous art—and not alone the literary. Carolino's use of another structure and other materials under what I might call the glaze of modern speech brings to mind the technique of our painters, under whose visual projections are buried the skeletons of divers remembered forms. Or again in our plays, in our middle-guard music, in our posh advertising, in our bedroom and studio manners, lurk the fossilized remains of, respectively, an earlier dramaturgy, a major-minor harmony, a compost of museum and library treasures, a set of gentlemanly and ladylike usages, all recast into the allusive enigmas of our day. That is what makes contemporary life so amusing. "I hope it," as our author says, "I not fear what the hail."

In the face of these truths, so easily seen and so clearly imparted, it will hardly be believed that there are people, institutions, lobbying groups that want to spoil the sport by reducing this life-giving fantasy to common prose. They maintain that even though we understand Carolino and he transports us by his genius, he writ no language. That was the charge against the divine Spenser, who survived it. Can Carolino and his disciples in our midst survive the onslaught of a reactionary rhetoric embodied in cocky manuals of usage and obese dictionaries? Take one of those in best repute: it says that "language is an indispensable instrument of human society," which strikes me as a paradox if language is a convention, as undoubtedly it is. How convene upon language if society does not preëxist? And then again, says the dictionary, "language is the means by which individuals understand each other." Don't we wish it were! The conclusion is perhaps sounder: something or other called "the effectiveness of human society" is declared to be "dependent upon the clarity, accuracy, and efficiency with which language is used or understood." But wouldn't "accuracy" here be greater if the sentence read "used *and* understood"?

Never mind! Here are thousands of words to be clear and accurate with. What do they do for the poetry of life as against the lexicographers' dreadful obsession with "individuals functioning as a community," with "modern man's functioning well in his society" and "keeping pace with the dynamic growth of his language"? *Whose* language? Why dynamic? How *growth*?

Once more, never mind! The words most of us use are all there, defined without any intrusion of elegance or wit such as ruined Dr. Johnson's reputation for seriousness. Many words are classified, some apparently by the Housing Commissioner, who calls them "substandard," like a tenement. And although the phrases or sentences illustrative of use do not lead the innocent very far, there are little essays on usage that explain why, for instance, *ain't* is logical but wrong for educated speakers in the non-jocular mood. It is odd, though, to find *like* as a conjunction sternly disallowed yet "hobbies *like* photography or painting" declared substandard. This vagary will only encourage people who say "I accepted the invitation as my wife."

No doubt our dictionary supplies enough words for the business of functioning and even of understanding one another. But that is not what makes the work obese and anti-literary. What swells the docket is that side by side with the mother tongue is a mass of mere *terms*: hundreds of scientific portmanteaus, to begin with, that cannot be sounded or spelled, but exist like the gold at Fort Knox, to back up if necessary the meaningless initials spoken among specialists; then many too many proper names, of men and places, with dates and population respectively attached. I do not mind *Fannie Farmer* or *Sauk Center*, both evocative of good things, but I grudge the space to *Orval Faubus* and *Momence, Ill.* (pop. 2949). ("When to the Momence of sweet silent thought. . . .") Besides, why is La Jolla not there? If a dictionary is to be also a desk encyclopedia, then it should take thought and give learning instead of the obvious. Forget *Paulette* as a girl's name and tell us it was a tax on officeholding under the old regime in France. And why, *why* the silliness and insufficiency of: "*Allyn*, a girl's given name; *Lundy*, a boy's given name"? Think of the old Latin grammar published by Allyn and Bacon, of the eminent shipwreckers established on Lundy. Do we have to be told in print that *Norm* is the diminutive of *Norman*, another "boy's given name"? I must say, the lack of imagination and the insistence on the needless in our technical (dynamic, functioning) civilization are at times beyond belief.

They can be illustrated even from the common-word entries in our chosen dictionary, already so overloaded. For example, what need of *écrasé*, *elinguation*, *eloign*, *embassador*, *furfuraceous*, followed a little later by a long list of *non*-words, many unreadable and some quite imaginary, for example, *non-astronomic*, *nonvaginal*, *non-Attic*, et cetera? It's a pity, too, that Churchill's unlucky *triphibious* should be accepted here and etymologized. It will only encourage the pedants, just as giving rights to *timewise* and *marketwise* will only encourage the ubiquitous *-wise* guys. As for sanctioning the illogical "water is *comprised* of hydrogen and oxygen," it will sooner or later lead to: "Electrolysis is a process by which water may be decomprised."

Apropos of definitions, the art of writing them is at a low ebb. Consider: "*A-Z test*, a test for determining the pregnancy of a woman by noting, etc.", when the meaning is "for determining whether a woman is pregnant;" and again: "*Nip and tuck*, in a race or contest, with one competitor equaling the speed or efforts of the other." The meaning of *with* in this last sentence can certainly not be found in the dictionary in which the sentence occurs. Nor does it seem fair to follow the physical definition of *paperback* with the words: "a book of this type . . . that is highly entertaining, sensational, or titillating, but has no literary value." Why, the publisher of this lexicon himself publishes dead and dying authors in paperback, and in the name of literature, not titillation.

On the whole, I think that these days we do less well with words and with paint than with sounds and with cameras. More of such poetry as is left in our souls has gone into the last pair, and the first is barren. We may think we pay equal attention to form and detail in all four arts, but neither practitioners nor beholders really do. The love of words and the passionate fantasy that animated Pedro Carolino are in eclipse. His devotion to helping conversation flourish had, thank God, no thought in it of society functioning or—obviously—of individuals straining to understand each other. His art fostered a spontaneous mating of minds across two, three, four languages, the fourth being his own unsurpassable creation. How Carolino achieved an immortality denied to us was not wholly the result of genius. He worked for it, as our productions show that we do not. We are lazy and our infancy lasts too long. This too he foresaw and warned us about in characteristic phrase and rhythm: "Apply you at the study during that you are young."

Le Faux Chic

A recent news story about a French dictionary of anglicisms, or more popularly of "Franglais," describes, no doubt accurately, the contents of the work and the views of its compilers. But it unwittingly gives a very misleading idea of what has happened and is happening to French, and in lesser measure to other Western languages, including English.

I am not here concerned to apply an epithet to the large-scale importation of Anglo-American vocables into French. Depending on one's feeling for words or vested interest in their use, one will find it acceptable, absurd, enriching, detestable, amusing, or immoral. But one thing it is not, and that is normal.

Languages, as everybody knows, have borrowed and exchanged words from time immemorial. But the examples and arguments given to suggest that Franglais is but a continuation of the happy practice err in both substance and judgment.

It is pointed out, for instance, that in the twelfth century the land-bound French took from the seafaring English the word *boat* and made it into *bateau*; so why be stiff-necked now and refuse *blue jeans*? The parallel is a gross misrepresentation. We are invited to believe that until the 1100s the French had listened to their mothers and not been near the water. The fact is that in the twelfth century the word *boat* did *not* exist in English but was current in both English and French in the form *bat*. It was a Germanic root and also a Celtic one (Kymri: *bâd*), and it spread all the way from Scandinavia to what is now Spain and Portugal.

Nor is this the whole story. The Old French of the twelfth century was not a language in the modern sense but a collection of dialects spoken in northern France, where Germanic tribes—notably the Franks and Normans—had settled. Their original speech had mingled with unstandardized, not-much-written forms of low Latin and Celtic patois. Along the facing coasts of England and France the language of the sea particularly would thrive on kindred roots.

The Norman Conquest of England in 1066 gave fresh occasions for crossing the channel and mixing vocabularies, and it was only after centuries—and the printing press—that something like two fairly unified national languages emerged, still very much mixed. As late as five hundred years after the Conquest, in the essays of Montaigne, the reader is struck by the dozens of words that sound deceptively "English"—*barguigner* (*bargain*) for instance, or *suburb(e)*.

These were good French and are no longer, because in the seventeenth and eighteenth centuries French underwent a purge to rid itself of words thought barbaric or foreign or pedantic or vulgar. With the purge came the excellent habit of turning all borrowings into French-looking words. Thus *riding-coat* became *redingote* and *bollwerk* became *boulevard*. (Incidentally, the *coat* in the former was a reborrowing, since *cotte* is Old French and modern too.)

Now compare this long evolution with what goes on among languages nowadays: in the early, formative span, a set of common roots and of cross-borrowings is followed by a gradual sifting and finally by standardization through printing. Borrowing and sifting were done semiconsciously, through speech and for use, by unassuming sailors, fishermen, merchants, soldiers, wandering students, and clerics. It was functional not bookish.

In our latter day, we find not true bookishness but its second-hand equivalent: the conscious, contrived prose of journalists and advertisers striving for novelty. Their effort is seconded by a kind of literacy that encourages every citizen to be clever and up to date in speech. Borrowings and inventions multiply not from practical need but from a low kind of snobbery.

That is plainly seen in Franglais. Those who combat it do not object because it borrows needed words, but because it throws into an established vocabulary words which duplicate native ones, e.g. *living* (with *room* omitted) for *studio*. Many of the numerous novelties are words that the native users cannot agree on how to pronounce—the French give *-ing* three different sounds. The terms, moreover, are used or made up contrary to their original sense (*un footing* is a walk, *un smoking* is a dinner jacket) and defy the common forms of handling: the gender, the plural, the combining, and often the spelling of Franglais words follow individual choice.

Whether taken as sad or funny, this state of affairs is a strictly modern achievement. It could not exist without our technology and our widespread semi-education. Uneducated people would shut their minds to such fancy tricks and continue to talk the vernacular. Better-educated people would resist out of a sense of fitness, aesthetic or intellectual. Nor does eventual assimilation seem possible, for what the users of these real or pseudo English words enjoy is just this outlandishness and anarchy of usage, this relief from the commonplace.

And that is the point at which Franglais represents in extreme form what is happening to most other civilized languages of the West. Bored by the barrage of common words for common use, we continually mix and stir vocabulary and usage, not to communicate but to refresh and enliven—indeed, to awaken. We borrow from the gutter and from high pedantry, misusing if we can, just to be sure the term is unusual. We wear out fancy metaphors as fast as we can make them, we rename things hoping they will look different. Even acronyms may express our desire for more mystery in life—and if so they succeed.

One word from Franglais may be taken as a symbol of the whole performance: *tennisman*. It is not and never was an

English word. (All the better, it's a creation!) What comes clear in it is *tennis*, which is what the English made, the old way, out of *tenez*, the warning word of the server in the old French game. *Tennis* then went back to France in the last century, and now *man* adds to it the charm of violating the normal nasalized pronunciation of *an*, besides going against the genius of French, which calls for *not* compounding ideas but articulating them—*joueur de tennis*. Now work out for yourself the state of mind, the emotional bent, that would make a native speaker of French prefer the compound—and judge that lost soul accordingly.

What Makes Writing Right?

Those who preach and teach "good writing" almost always appeal to the need for "communication." They urge the fact that writing is to be read, and when read, understood. And if the particular piece of writing is intended as "a scientific communication," the precept seems all the more apt and imperative. The phrase scientific communication was in fact established from the earliest days of scientific journals and meetings to make clear that in modern science the practitioners do not keep their findings secret; they tell what they know, for the benefit of other workers and ultimately of humankind.

But it is clear today that this appeal, this tearful plea to communicate, repeatedly voiced by the critics of scientific writing, does little good. The staffs of learned journals have to edit and rewrite more and more of what they receive, while keen observers of the scene such as Dr. Lois DeBakey and the late Franz Ingelfinger, editor of *The New England Journal of Medicine*, carry on a veritable crusade for "communication."

Now it is fair to assume that nobody writes a paper so as to conceal his work; there are no alchemists around giving out false clues to secret formulas. Every piece published or unpublished tries to communicate. If it fails, urging the need will not improve the paper or the general situation. Writers muddle their meaning because they are unable to see and hear their words as these will look and sound to the receiving mind; they have not learned to impersonate the reader.

Nor will remembering and applying rules of grammar be of much help by itself. The difficulty goes beyond mere correctness. What is needed is a form of deliberate self-consciousness, detaching oneself from what one has put down on paper and comparing it—with what? If one can't imagine the reader and his stubborn little mind, what else is there? After scanning the state of professional writing for half a century I have come to think that for many writers there may be a better target than "effective communication," with its implied guessing at the mind of another. A preferable aim, I suggest, is "fit expression," by which I mean something like the work of the artist working from a model. Let the writer ask himself: is this really what I did, what I saw, what I found, what I conclude? If his word portrait is a good likeness, he will automatically communicate. And this indirect way to his goal—copying the model—has a great advantage: it gives him two known objects to match as closely as possible: the reality he remembers and the words he is setting down or scratching out.

The task still calls for self-consciousness, on a double front: What was the experiment really like? What do these words really mean? But in place of the vague, distant mind of the unknown reader, there is now a vivid experience of one's own to force the necessary questioning of every word. In short, the work of revision now has a compelling pattern. Like the portraitist, the writer puts in lines and takes them out until he is satisfied with the likeness between his work and the subject.

To be sure, this reorientation from "communicating" to "fit expression" takes us only part of the way. How does the writer come to see the *un*likeness between his experimental results and the words he has chosen? A first step is to keep the report a little while before sending it out. Reread it, say, two weeks after it is "finished," and you the author will find some passages incomprehensible, or at best clumsy description. Next you must adopt standard procedures, as if your were doing a physiological titration—or making tea. Here are some:

First and most important: TRANSLATE. I mean by this re-place every current jargon phrase by the word for its root idea: learning experience = learning; teaching profession = teachers;

weather conditions = weather; time factor = time; meaningful relationship = love affair (or friendship); precipitation = rainfall; nutritional routine = eating habits; of a calcareous nature = chalky.

Those bad words, like *paradigm* (= model) and *parameter* (= limits), are from common prose and common speech, where new vocables sprout incessantly and are used obsessively. Each scholarly and scientific specialty suffers from additional words, which pass for technical terms, though they are not. Get rid of them and the effect will be to lay bare what you have actually said. It is then easier to notice gaps in thought, insufficient or repetitious details, apparent contradictions, needless variants, and all the other faults writing is liable to.

Next, the writer seeking to model his prose on reality will take pains to CUT DOWN ON ABSTRACT WORDS, even if they are good words. Watch for the strings of nouns in *-tion, -ity*, and *-ment* held together by *of, to, with*, and other prepositions. "The measurement of the material was effected by obtention of the ratio of assimilation to retention of an assignment that was initially calibrated for difficulty of absorption." Even worse is the piling up of words without clear joints between: "premature unauthorized partial disclosure."

There is a conventional belief that in the sciences the abstract mode is traditional and desirable; it keeps the tone impersonal and conveys the mood of objectivity. But if the abstract manner is used so that all it yields is error and confusion, it had better be abandoned. Too often, abstraction is resorted to for impressiveness, which the pared down and concrete style is thought to lack. The answer to that is: what will truly impress is the scientific work itself, nothing else.

At any rate, with the Thing Said shown in sharp contour by the use of simple and direct words, two good results may be counted on: grammar is more easily repaired and nonsense reveals itself. Here are two examples of blunders involving grammar and sense: "Due to a printing error, the enclosed poster replaces the one previously sent." "The conference has been called to discuss better industrial products as a contribution to the country's economic problems." The obvious commands here are: BREAK IT UP and LOOK FOR THE ABSURD: "The printer made an error. The enclosed poster replaces, etc." And: "The conference has been called to discuss, etc. . . . It should contribute to the *solution* of the country's problems."

The thoughtful will note that in these two cases the underlying questions were: What did happen? What will happen? Each of the objects to be portrayed in words, when squarely looked at, compelled its fit expression.

Pitfalls

Look for Trouble Ahead

George Orwell pointed out years ago that bad writing was often a sign of political deceit. Today it is a sign of unlovely human traits as well—vanity, pretentiousness, complacency about one's ignorance, disrespect toward the listener, and a curious mixture of slavish imitation and a desire to appear original.

The urge to be original and up to the minute expresses itself in neologisms—newly made-up words and new meanings thrust on old, usually distinctive, words. There is nothing wrong with the new as such. The question is, does this particular novelty fill a need, add a nuance? And: will it last, or turn yellow and be swept away like last summer's leaves? Finally, is it fit by its shape and sound to join the great company of English words?

A good new word for a truly new thing should sound as if it had been born, not pieced together out of shavings and leftovers. For example, *clone* is good, because, though derived from the Greek for *twig*, it is short, does not show off a learned ancestry and, its meaning once grasped, is unmistakable. And of course it was needed as soon as genetically duplicate creatures could be produced.

Vanity, always restless, causes people to coin or combine words for which there is no need. Out of the nursing profession has come *wellness* to replace *health*, on the dubious ground that *health* can be qualified—poor health, failing health—whereas *wellness* is not variable. But words in *-ness* are a last resort; when *sloth* was commonplace there was no need of *laziness*. *Health* deserves its monopoly.

New words in *-ize* belong to the same unfortunate class. They are coined to suggest a process—the heroic, scientific conquest of mind over matter. Their effect is to break up all of life into separate, labeled, impersonal techniques (*personalize, finalize*), of which there is no end; a fresh example, *laymanize*, turns out to mean simply "make more readable."

Nor is *-ize* the only way by which pretentious people make "process verbs." The National Institute of Mental Health (not yet Mental Wellness) promotes the Search for Alternative Pursuits. First we are told that " 'alternative' is not just a synonym for 'substitute,' since it implies being more satisfactory and not merely a replacement." This distinction is imaginary— why not say Preferable Pursuits and cut the explanation? But wait! We are further urged: "Exercise your capacity for *alternativing*." Query: is it pronounced *-tivving* or *-tyving*?

It should be pronounced detestable, and a prayer uttered against the temptation to *verbify* (an example of what not to do). The wretched verbs spawn new nouns, equally bad: the Postal Service announces a program of *route demotorization*, which a thoughtful critic insists should be *repedestrianization*.

In weighing the merits of a new word or phrase, or the new extension of an old one, it is imperative to think ahead. The experienced writer—or speaker, for that matter—knows that the misuse or abuse of words brings on troubles not immediately apparent. The blithe venture leads to a form, a sense, or a combination that is ambiguous, puzzling, or ludicrous.

Such an opportunity to think ahead was missed when someone launched the vogue of the now popular *acerbic*. English has long had the Latinate adjective *acerb*, meaning sharp; but according to the apologists of the new bastard form, "it didn't sound like an adjective, so *-ic* was tacked on." Of course, *superb* is an adjective and felt to be such by most people. Are we going to be faced with *superbic*?

Thinking ahead, one sees what will happen when *acerbic* calls for its noun: it will have to be *acerbicity*, like *public*, *publicity*; *catholic, catholicity,* and so on. But we already have a noun correctly formed from the true adjective—*acerbity*. So by using *acerbic* we open the way to a silly long word, bypass a compact old one, and expose ourselves to having editors "correct" *acerbity* for lacking a syllable.

Looking still farther ahead, one sees looming the dislodging of *exacerbate* by *exacerbicate*. Already *acerbic* has given *acidic* a foothold ("*acidic* rain") and the *acidic test* awaits us. But this is to double the offense, for *acidic* has a genuine technical use; it means not *acid* but *acid-forming*. Hence *acid rain* and *acid remarks* are not *acidic*. Anyhow, there was no need to bring into common use the rather literary *acerb* unless one knew its origin and true shape. We had *sharp, cutting, sarcastic,* to be going on with.

The manufacturers of the new have another obligation that they usually forget: a new word should be sayable. Among recent innovations two at least flout this requirement. How does one utter *parenting*? The accent has to fall on the first syllable, but that muffles the proper sound of the second, and the result is a nasal rendition of *parroting*. (Besides, we had the perfectly clear *parentage*.) Even worse is the verb *mentoring*, which has popped up in business circles where some women think they need a mentor in order to succeed (from the *New York Times*: "upward, downward, and outward mentoring.") Now *mentor* is a spondee (equal stress on each syllable); does it become men*tor*'ing and lose audible connection with its origin? Or does it lose it the other way by rhyming with *entering*?

Again, there was no need for either verb; their very aim is harmful. Reducing human actions to processes by mere words is misplaced sociology; it turns one's sense of individual life into the vacuum of statistical life: it *anonymizes* you!

Promiscuous Pairs

A letter from the White House does not come for me in every mail, so when one arrived a while ago, I read it with care. It was a two-page circular, signed "Jimmy," which urged me to support his policy about a troubled area so as to "help assure continuing peace."

This use of *assure* for *insure* shows that the President reads the papers and follows their lead. Until quite recently, the distinction was clear and automatic. One *assured* one's friends of one's regard and *insured* by suitable acts that they believed one's assurances. (Some writers, by the way, make a further distinction by writing *in*sure and *en*sure to separate the literal from the figurative use—goods are insured, results or success ensured. Since the difference in pronunciation is rarely made or not perceptible, this nuance of spelling seems superfluous.) In any case, *assure*, like *reassure*, is directed at persons and relies mainly on words. *Insure* aims at a state of things and implies taking steps to make sure: You insure your privacy by shutting the door, your safety by turning off the motor, and world peace by various means beyond fair words.

It is true that one or two venerable corporations bear names that seem to disregard the difference, notably the Equitable Life Assurance Society. Perhaps they mean to assure you that you're insured. At any rate, the distinction has come into being and is worth preserving; it marks off important shades of meaning: Assurance without insurance is hot air.

"But why fuss? The distinction is out-of-date—everybody uses the words interchangeably."

"If you think so, let me *insure* you that you are wrong."

Similar pairs, when miscast as they often are today, may not create so much trouble but inevitably blur meanings. *Infer* and *imply*, for example, confuse something thought with something said. The speaker or writer who implies has "folded up" an idea in his remarks (or possibly his actions) and it is for the reader or listener to pull it out again by inferring that it is there. Surely detective fiction has taught us to *infer* extensively from clues—such as (to borrow from Conan Doyle) "how far the parsley had sunk into the butter upon a hot day."

Another common confusion we could do without is that between *verbal* and *oral*: "Trouble is, he had no contract, only a verbal agreement." The intended meaning is: Nothing was written down. This ambiguity is common; one hears it even from the Supreme Court bench, where a bit of precision would not seem out of place. *Verbal* means in, of, or about words. (Incidentally, an exchange of spoken promises can be a contract too, but that's not the point here.) *Verb*, *verbiage*, *verbalize* all show that the root says nothing about speaking or writing. *Oral* is needed to tell us which. It means for, from, in, about, or by way of the mouth: an oral antiseptic. So an oral agreement is one kind of verbal agreement—the spoken kind—whereas a nod of assent is neither oral nor verbal.

Those vagrant words are so ordinary and useful that there is no avoiding them and it is a waste and failure of sense to misuse them. But many other pairs, which occur just as often in speech and print, show that different words do, after all, make a difference. Not long ago a film being made under the title *Perversity* had to be renamed, because of a fear among its makers that it would suggest *perversion*, instead of the actual theme, which was the stubborn, self-centered behavior of a pair of lovers. Again, consider *precipitous* and *precipitate*. Both mean the opposite of gradual, and good writers have long associated the first with space and the second with time— a precipitous slope, a precipitate act. Does the choice matter? Yes, it does. "His fall was precipitous" connotes a physical drop from a height. Put *precipitate* and what is suggested is not only a short span of time but also a different meaning of fall, the figurative one—fall from high office.

There is, of course, no need to use either word. Plenty of adjectives are at hand waiting for modern man to use them spontaneously—*quick, rapid, hasty, hurried, swift*; and *steep, sharp, abrupt, headlong, breakneck*. And these make for better prose, in addition to being the right word. It should not be hard to renew acquaintance with them and postpone "precipitous decisions" indefinitely.

The same caution and remedy apply to *perspicuous* and *perspicacious*—when in doubt, drop 'em. The first means capable of being seen through; and the other, capable of seeing through, with the connotation of *wise, shrewd, perceptive*. Why not say just that and damn highfalutin? There will always be enough pedants and show-offs left to confound usage and, as a result, make exact reading and writing harder than it already is.

What reinforces this complaint about the use of long and learned words is the prevalence of an entirely different kind of pair, the kind that marks no difference but duplicates, badly, what we already have words for. A new term is needless. Take the familiar companion of every journey on the highway, the *median divider*. The name is to be condemned on the face of it as unnatural. Imagine yourself designing a broad high-speed road. What will you do to keep down the number of head-on collisions? You will leave a wide strip of ground between the lines of cars. Where will that strip be? In the middle, of course. It is thus the *middle strip*, or better, the *center strip*, because "middle" vaguely suggests two other strips and the travel lanes are not strips. There is only one strip, in the center—the *center strip* (or *fence* if one is used instead).

That, surely, is how a plain mind thinks, or would think if not corrupted by the steady flood of out-of-the-way expressions for simple things. Any fool can think of leaving a center strip down the road, but "to provide a median divider, continuous except for approved interchanges" (not "crossovers," mind you)—that sounds as if the whole faculty of M.I.T. had taken a hand in the *design creation*.

Notice, too, that besides the flummery of the phrase, each of the terms is miscast. *Median* is not the same as *middle* or *center* ("He likes to occupy the median of the stage"?). And to *separate* speeding cars is not the same as to *divide* them (a "cream divider"?). Now the puzzle of the age is how, given the passion for these bastard growths, we managed to get such excellent new terms as *jet lag, ballpoint pen,* and *seat belt*.

Tonier than Thou

I always look forward to the Saturday *New York Times*, because it is the slimmest of the week. The stories are shorter and terser, as if the newsmen were working with genius unleashed to make sure of their day off. But that noble compression does not prevent other people, whom the newspaper quotes, from showing off their usual tricks. Some Saturdays ago, in the business section, I came across this typical remark: "The acquiring company will research the full operations of the clothing company to determine 'what the synergies are with our own apparel business.' "

Note first the pomposity of *research* and *determine*, used for *look into* and *decide*, but necessary to lead up to *synergies*, the goal, the summit, the glorification of the act by which two companies will intermingle their three-piece suits.

The urge these days to be technical, scientific, about everything seems irresistible. It is the royal road to being high-toned, chock-full of prestige. Those who sell need that cachet (*Isotoner* gloves, *SyberVision NeuroMuscular Programming*). But one cannot blame the shopkeepers and advertisers alone: they have only encouraged, not created, the public's conviction that anything described in familiar terms is ordinary, negligible. What the buyer wants from goods is mystery and miracles, and these are best suggested by technical words half understood.

What are in fact them there *synergies*? The original coinage from Greek roots meaning "to act with" was *synergism*. It was needed in medicine to mean an effect produced by two or more drugs and that differed from their separate effects. Some-body then derived *synergy* (and, God help us, *synergize*) to mean combine(d) efforts—coöperation. The peculiar idiocy of *synergies*, in the plural, is that *syn* already denotes joint action for enhanced results. Those two clothing companies will turn into a black hole if they don't moderate their $E = mc^2$.

Our ordinary talk is already stuffed with vocables that flout common sense to no purpose except sounding uncommon—*radiothon*, *sportagon*, *cargomation* and other ungainly dino-saurs with *-thon*, *-tron*, *-matic* and *auto-*, *hydro(a)-*, or *perma-* at head and tail. A fact to ponder: For half a century the people and the schools have agreed that Greek and Latin were stone dead and of no earthly use. During the same half cen-tury the people and the unschooled have messed about with Greek and Latin scraps to replace good English words with hybrid forms.

During the same time, the Graeco-Latin vocabulary of grammar and rhetoric has been ransacked for obscure terms that could shed a little glamour on workaday things. *Metaphor* has been stretched to cover so many disparate ideas that it no longer carries any clear sense. *Parameter*, *paradigm*, *interface*, *empathy*, *quantum* (leap or jump) are in the same condition. And it was only by prompt individual action that the world escaped the infliction of *synecdoche*. The story is instructive and for once has a happy ending.

This absurdity was hatched in a report of the Senate Select Committee on Intelligence, which stated that certain assassina-tion plots by government agencies had been "concealed by synecdoche." (Picture the senators goggling.) The word means naming a part to indicate the whole—"thirty sails" for "thirty ships." Fortunately, a column in a Washington paper rid us of the new menace. The pedant who filched the word from its proper place was obviously unable to see that if a part is made to stand for the whole, it does not conceal but points out.

As for *quantum*, the ignorance is even more flagrant. The users believe the jump is sudden and big and implies some sort of improvement. Makers of gadgets daily propose to "quantum leap into the 21st century." The fact is, a quantum jump is neither large nor sudden but simply discontinuous. The electron that jumps does not pass through the space between its orbit and the next; it disappears from the one and reappears in the other, emitting a photon (light) in so doing. Clearly, the image is applicable only to a stage magician.

The scientists, of course, are not responsible for our antics, but they too can be bitten by the desire to seem, as well as be, scientific. Thus some hospitals and medical journals have banned *x-ray*. It is now a *roentgenogram*, noun and verb. Ask the staff who Wilhelm Röntgen was and see them stare. As for the pronunciation, with *antigen* and *carcinogen* flying about, you can guess what's coming—Runtjenogram. Apparently it was worth the effort to have got rid of a word everyone understood and could speak and spell.

These many pedantries, which soil the language with as many mouldy spots, make one long for a cleansing bath—and that, alas, reminds me of the beauty specialist who announces: "I'll oxygenate your skin with a spray of steam—and your skin will never forget it." Truth in advertising at last—if the spray really *is* steam.

Page Mrs. Malaprop

Who is she?—the governess in Sheridan's play *The Rivals*, who uses big words that she does not understand and that she confuses with others of similar sound. She says *epitaphs* for *epithets*. Among writers and critics of language her name is now standard as a tag for mistakes in the meaning of words. Some linguists do not acknowledge the existence, or even the possibility, of such mistakes. Why not? Because some malaprops have made their way by usage into correctness—for example, *restive*, which now means uneasy, rest*less*, whereas its original sense is stubborn and *at rest*. Some therefore maintain that any new blunder should have an equal opportunity to become respectable. As we saw on an earlier page, one extremist believes that "no native speaker can make a mistake."

One might ask why the privilege is limited to natives, but meantime, most people, native and foreign, want to be sure of meanings in what they hear and read. It is annoying—and often ludicrous—when a malaprop jumps out at you in the middle of serious discourse. Thus the college president who said, "We want to give everybody who comes to us a *fulsome* education," cast doubt on the quality of his establishment.

Malaprops arise from careless listening and hasty reading, coupled with the false notion that one can always "figure out" what an unfamiliar word means. *Fulsome* does not mean full or complete, and *noisome* has nothing to do with noise. In a recent issue of a usually well-edited weekly of opinion, it is said apropos of a political campaign, "From an unexpected quarter comes a major kudo for" So-and-so. The writer saw *kudos* (*fame*, in the useless Greek language) and took it for a plural. He inferred a ridiculous singular and made it stand for "one more stroke of favor or popularity."

This type of reasoning is fatal. Language is not an algebra, in which the symbols can be handled freely without changing their meaning. In language, the sense of the simplest elements can vary widely. Take *in-*: *inopportune* says *not* opportune, but *inflammable* does not say *not* flammable—on the contrary —and as a result the word has had to be replaced by *flammable* to save the lives of those who guess at words from their parts.

Malaprops betray not just ignorance but also the vulgar desire to be stylish beyond one's means. If the author of "major kudo" had remained his normal, lovable self, he would have written simply "a big boost to So-and-so's prestige." For the use of *major* is also an affectation, albeit a very usual one. That vogue word takes the place of *big*, *great*, *important*, *large*, *sizable*, *leading*, *conspicuous*, and other adjectives, each of which would raise a sharper image than *major*.

Like *major*, which was only a show-off word when it started on its way, some malaprops suddenly burst into general use, as if in answer to a widespread longing for the strange un-known. A recent case is *testament*. For centuries it has had only the meaning embodied in the phrase "last will and testa-ment," or by clear extension, "legacy," as in *The Testament of Beauty*, and of course the Old and the New Testaments. Lately it has usurped the place of *testimony*, *witness*, *tribute*, and quickly fallen into a mere synonym for *indication* and *sign*. "The new national holiday is a testament to the man who led the civil rights movement" (editorial). "A wonderful testa-ment to her talent and beauty" (movie critic). By echo, per-haps, *fundament* is appearing in displacement of *foundation*, which clearly shows the urge to give up the known and tried for the venturesome. "That event was the fundament of Polish nationalism." Those who look up the accepted meaning of this impostor will be shocked to the bottom of their souls.

Other absurd miscarriages of sense are caused by the ignorant use of *mundane, volatile, avid, ameliorate, fervent, evasive, cohort, coalesce, credulity, immodest, legendary.* (See the chart "Exercise in Discretion," p. 77.)

In any issue of a daily or weekly journal one can cull half a dozen malaprops, original or quoted. The Mayor of New York, for example, has picked up *pristine* (no doubt from one of his constituents) and used it twice in an interview on his winning the primary: "I'm not going to tell you that everything I've done was the most pristine." And again: "So whatever I do, I'm going to take the most pristine and doable."

Now *pristine* is related to the Latin *primus*; it means first or early, and by extension fresh, unspoiled. A pristine copy of a book has not been smudged by handling. The contorted idea in the present misuse is: not dictated by self-seeking political motives. But this vague intimation of "pure" is too far off usage to be tolerable. In any case, "most pristine" is as bad as "most unique."

With *legend(ary)*, the trouble is radical ambiguity. A legend is a story without basis in fact. What then are we to think of "This silk lingerie is fast becoming a legend"? Or, "W.S. offers you a legend," which turns out to be an expensive brandy? The intention is to persuade us that here are famous, extraordinary products, but perhaps the brandy's excellence *is* a legend, a myth, and surely it is only Lady Godiva's negligée that was legendary.

So beware of malaprops. To repeat a suggestion often used by conference chairmen after greeting a panel: "Now I'll leave you to coagulate your thoughts."

Vulgar, Vulgarity, Vulgarisms

One of Shakespeare's often quoted maxims is almost always misapplied. "One touch of nature makes the whole world kin" is taken to mean that a hint of simple goodness brings out universal sympathy. This is far off the mark. Instead, as the context shows, the meaning is: There is a trait common to everybody, which is vulgarity: "All with one consent praise new-born gauds," i.e. the new, showy, and shoddy—"dust that is a little gilt."

It can be argued that vulgarity has the merit of keeping us aware of our wretched humanity, saving us from any self-conceit based on our knowledge, our accomplishments, our elegant tastes and virtuous opinions. At any rate, an honest soul, after due self-survey, will acknowledge its liability to vulgar thought, feeling, or behavior. The argument is practically circular: Vulgar, from *vulgus*, the crowd, denotes what is common, and in turn gives to the adjective "common" its pejorative meaning. It is a tacit recognition that the best in anything is a scarce commodity.

But unlike "common," "vulgar" has many shades of meaning. The vulgar words that a polite person does not permit himself in the worst of quarrels differ from the (supposedly) vulgar taste for pork and beans, and this again from such vulgar genteelisms as saying *commence* for *begin* or pronouncing *issue* and *tissue* "issyou" and "tissyou." In short, vulgarity is a movable beast which bites different people at different levels of their being.

Similarly, it has varied in various ages. Nowadays, language that is crude, rough, or even gross is not reproved as it once was; and though snobbish affectation about music and art is rampant, it often includes in its top-loftiness certain forms of the low *and* vulgar, dignified for the occasion by such terms as "camp" or "pop." This leaves as the reprehensibly vulgar the habits and usages of people who thoughtlessly follow the crowd and take up all "new-born gauds" without discrimination, not seeing "dust" when it is "gilt."

The upshot is that in addition to all errors, ambiguities, nonsense, malaprops, and highfalutin, ordinary speech and writing is marred by these gauds, these recurrent vulgarisms. Some are just tasteless, others sound pretentious, all are kept alive by the copycat instinct. A list of vulgarisms can only be indicative, not exhaustive and, like an anthology, it is bound to arouse objections: "You've left out such and such and you had the gall to put in THIS!" Never mind! Take, on a ten-day free trial, my partial alphabet (partial in both senses) and if dissatisfied, make up one of your own.

ALL THAT. "They say it's a good movie but it's not all that good." This British expression is one of those imports that this country could do without.

AS OF. "It hasn't been confirmed as of yet," said Mr. Gorbachev. "As of now, I'm still using my own teeth." Go jump into the Sea of Azov! *Yet* and *now* by themselves are the decent usage.

AUTHOR HEMINGWAY. Every author, acrobat, bank teller, or town clerk is first and always a man or woman, and only at times a practitioner of some trade or profession. *Time*-style vulgarity started the practice of labeling people in this servile way—Clarinettist Beppo Lento. Only titles are proper as labels—doctor, captain, senator, and so on. It only costs a *the* to be courteous: "*the* actress Helen Hayes"—if you knew her, you'd know there are hours and hours when she is not acting.

DATES AND DATING (not in the courting sense). The

established usage is: "The work dates from (not *to*) 1583"; or: "is dated 1583," which is matched by: "The experts date it 1583," (again not *to*). But the recent perverseness of "dating to" is a trifle compared to the violation of a useful rule about dates preceding nouns as modifiers: Her 1972 fall from a horse,/his 1916 struggle with polio, and so on. To a good reader, such expressions imply a regular series of similar events—yearly falls from the horse and bouts of polio. "The 1891 edition of *Huckleberry Finn*" means that there are other editions with different dates, just like "the September issue of *The Atlantic*" or "the 1986 appearance of Halley's Comet." The new error misleads when we read of "the 1920 marriage of Countess Haha," because it suggests repeated marriages at various dates. The source of this vulgar practice is doubtless the legitimate one followed in scientific journals: "In his 1905 paper on relativity. . . ." Einstein wrote other papers, before and after. Even so, it would be more elegant to say: "In his paper of 1905. . . . " Give us a little "of."

FOR INSTANCE (NOUN). "What are some of the for instances in each of those business categories?" The interviewer meant only: "Please name some cases," for that is what the financial analyst went on to do.

HONORABLE. Senator Byrd recently pointed out that this appellation calls for *Mr.* or *Robert* or *Senator* between it and his last name. "The honorable Byrd" is a vulgarism, and so is "the Reverend Jones." The curtailed form ranks with "Sir Raleigh." On the other hand, it is foolish to say: "My name is Mrs. Brown." *Mrs.* is not part of anybody's name. The choice is "I am Mrs. Brown" or "my name is Emily Brown." All these things used to come naturally to everybody—what's come over us to make the whole world so kin?

-ITIS. This Latin suffix used in medicine means inflammation, as every chump can figure out from *appendicitis* and *tonsillitis*. Why that chump says "Churchillitis" when he means that he admires the late statesman and collects all writings about him passes understanding. Nor can the compound be used to criticize another's hobby, e.g. "baseballitis." If you are rude enough to impute a disease, there's always *mania* and *obsession*.

NO PROBLEM. To substitute this phrase invariably for *yes, certainly, of course, with pleasure* (*not* "my pleasure"), and similar forms of assent is a vulgar habit, apt to irritate the listener. Its negative, equally to be avoided, is "no way."

PERSONIFICATION. What is aimed at here is the practice of turning the names of places and institutions into persons by adding the possessive *'s*: Illinois' governor, Yale's Giamatti, the nation's capital. This is another of (shall I say?) *Time*'s misdeeds, done for the sake of that knowingness and brevity that are the essence of the vulgar. The *national* capital, the *governor of* Illinois, and Mr. Giamatti *of Yale* are the recognizable entities. So little did Yale own Mr. Giamatti that he left the place when he felt like it. For other parts of aggregates use the simple apposition: the Columbia campus, the Ford factory—keeping the apostrophe-s strictly for friends and relatives.

THIS DESK. A sense of deference and modesty makes nice people avoid too frequent a use of the pronoun *I*. But avoiding it can be overdone so that it unwittingly draws attention to the ego. In articles and books, one encounters *this writer*, which is clumsy, and elsewhere *this desk, this office, this column*, which are absurd. In the nature of things, those pieces of furniture can have no opinions or desires, and the slowest reader will detect a live creature under the false cover. In a letter, *I* is often the only sensible word to begin with. It's a genteelism to resist the rule: "an I for an I."

UPCOMING. Responding to words with an instant image has its penalties: whenever I read about an *upcoming* play or book I see it as vomited—rejected—out of some great maw. On feebler days it seems as if hoisted by a dumbwaiter. *Forthcoming* is the older word, and preferable because free of the suggestion red-hot, up-to-the-minute, just as in its twin, *ongoing*, the taint is the implication of steady, noble industry.

YOU NAME IT. Tiresome when frequent, and offensive like an impertinent nudge, this final term of enumeration is no better than the *what have you* which it displaced.

VISIT WITH. Years ago, A. A. Milne wondered why the suspect in crime fiction always "effected an egress" when he might just as easily go out. Likewise, it is surely as easy to visit one's grandmother as to visit *with* her. "Mayor Visits With Homeless," says a recent headline. Perhaps the *with* is meant to show that he did not rush through but lingered and chatted. But *visiting* may be short or long, and *with* implies a reciprocity contrary to fact. When you visit your grandmother, *she* isn't visiting *you*.

WHAT YOU'RE SAYING IS . . . If you feel superior to the person you're talking to, try to conceal or—better—forget it; don't in any case utter these introductory words. They are so patronizing that they justify one's breaking in with: "What I am saying is what I have just said—I don't need your help."

In printed matter, certain habits of our time display its inexhaustible vulgarity. The first and worst is the use of initialese and acronyms. They are barely tolerable in speech; when they are made up at will by successive writers to cosset their laziness, their childishness equals their vulgarity. (See below, pp. 147–48, a way to do without and restore clarity.)

Points in Passing

Just discovered, by numerous people at the same time: students cannot be taught how to write well, except by having them write. (*New York Times*, April 14, 1986.) Putting checkmarks in little squares so as to match a set of words with a set of definitions does not work, nor filling in blanks in prepared sentences, or any other device of objective tests. Those of us who said the same thing forty years ago, in our youth, were denounced as reactionaries bent on obstructing the march of mind; we were esthetes ignorant of the *science* of testing, which can frame questions statistically guaranteed effective: they discriminate the able from the incompetent, and they are also perfectly fair, since no individual judgment goes into the numerical grade.

In the years since that first discovery, now upset by the recent one, I have noticed again and again that especially able writers among my students would fail the objective writing test required for admission to law school. There is in the checkmark use of the mind something contrary to the act of writing. When I have myself tried to fill in blanks in a paragraph composed by someone else, I have found the effort very great; I needed more time than I could afford were I taking the test in reality.

What all this means is that writing is something that must well up from within like a flowing spring. It may come in spurts, but unless the ability to utter is nurtured by practice and guided by comment, no skill and speed at picking out "right answers" will make up for it. Even the vocabulary-matching will be a dead loss, since the words have not been used *for a purpose*. All writing is purposive, and a purpose must be genuinely felt or it is not—purposive.

Besides harming the student, so-called objective tests of writing also handicap the teacher. How can one improve the learner's prose if the learner does not produce any? The violin teacher does not content himself with playing, to show off dexterity or illustrate mistakes—he must see and hear the instrument *being played*. In student writing, when the assignments are frequent and well designed, all kinds of error and clumsiness occur that are never found in the sample sentences of manuals and grammar books. These faults have the advantage of being genuine; they represent somebody's ways of thought, and finding them faulty is a therapeutic attack on the mind that produced them. I speak of faults because they are likely to be many, but student writing also contains happy turns and subtle thoughts, which by being praised further the arduous training. In short, with a live author there is an emotional involvement between teacher and taught which serves them both.

Nobody concerned with the written word can form views useful to himself or anybody else without close acquaintance with bad writing. It is in the bad that, paradoxically, the principles of the good find their justification: it is better to do *this*, because if you don't, the result will be *that*—ambiguity, self-contradiction, false lead, wrong emphasis, or some other impediment to the reader's understanding. Under a noticing eye, student writing yields lessons whose value lies in showing reasons for the teacher's way, as against the student's natural faith that whatever he has set down conveys his meaning. Points in passing—more points than anyone can remember—are the means by which one learns how to improve one's writing and how to help others with theirs.

A friend of mine, who occasionally sends me instances of what he calls the new pidgin, let me have a memo from the hospital to which he is attached. The paper is headed: *Payroll*

Pend: "This is to notify you that the payroll for the period April 21 through 25 will be pended until the following week." What bright lad, one wonders, thought that one up? Did he think that *suspend* (or *hold up*) was too long a word? Did he fail to catch the full sense of *pending*, which contains the idea of a future decision to be made? Or have the computer boys ruled that when they change their systems (for that was the reason given) everything pends? Everybody knows that they are by nature independent and garble as they go.

But one folly does not make a madhouse, and what is depressing about this particular innovation is that it brings to mind a series of misdeeds, all very recent, which threaten the integrity of verbs. I refer to the blurring of the difference between transitive and intransitive. An intransitive verb is one that "does not go across" to its object—it stays within the subject: "She *appeals* by her expression"/ "the poor child *languished* through the summer"/ "they *strolled* agreeably along the boardwalk." As soon as someone, heedless of what he hears and reads, begins to say: "they strolled the boardwalk," the intransitive is turned into a transitive, which sounds illiterate to anybody familiar with good usage.

Lately, we have seen common verbs shift in both directions: people say that so-and-so has "converted to Catholicism;" or that his success "culminates a long effort." The first example makes a transitive into an intransitive and the second does the reverse. Here are other examples culled from the press within a week: Cunard Princess (a ship) departs Acapulco/ denounced those who are helping to inflame/ both graduated college/ proposal on which I consulted in 1976/ a desire to reconcile with the Church/ he intends to defend against them/ residents on the coast refused to evacuate/ this translates to the same thing/ the probation officer said that he programs well (i.e. obeys the rules of the program). And of course the incessant "it boggles the mind," which should be: "the mind boggles."

But why not change and change about? One reason, never

to be forgotten, is that a novelty should justify itself. What good purpose, not previously taken care of, is served by this license to switch indications? A second reason is the ambiguous result. "He programs well" had to be explained from the context. Then there is the "trouble later on" discussed on an earlier page. If one simply *defends* against opponents, self-defense, she defended herself, become redundant. If one consulted on a proposal, meaning gave advice, how avoid confusion when one means I consulted (an expert)—i.e. *took* advice? The hesitation as to what is meant may be momentary, but any stoppage of meaning is a nuisance, especially when the causes of it are multiplied by others' ignorance or indifference.

Finally, there is in these changes a crass lack of regard for pleasant shades of thought and feeling. If we walk the streets, why shouldn't we stroll them? Because strolling has no object—the play on the word *object* makes my point. If you convert to oil heat, why not to Catholicism? Because in the first case, your house or furnace is clearly understood; hence you must have a comparable object in the second—convert your self or your friend or your soul, which it is trivializing to leave out. In the reverse instances, the intransitive idea is the very thing that matters: an appealing expression appeals *to* everybody—the spectators are not being processed. Think of what is threatened: "Novels like this appeal many readers." Disgusting, no? So is the new usage; let it pend forever.

Knowing the standard meaning of words has advantages other than the bland feeling of conformity (the counterpart of the crude feeling of dissent). I remember a charming lighthearted novel in which the character of a superficially amiable old man was nicely indicated by his replying to all requests: "Presently, my dear, presently." To those who know the word only in the meaning of "right now," the phrase was unintelligible, so it never conveyed the old man's smooth selfishness. Recently, Mr. William Safire, the eminent speech-gatherer, who knows what a word's worth, resolved to be independent of modernism and declared for the classic use of *presently* to mean *soon.** The decision is worthy, but *soon* is not quite what *presently* means. It is far less definite, and thereby a wonderful aid to postponement—"in a little while, my dear, when you've forgotten what you asked for, I'll have forgotten it too and will never get around to doing it."

Rather more serious, for literary purposes, is the loss of *disinterested.* Just think of the climax of Shaw's *Doctor's Dilemma*, when the likable, capable Doctor Ridgeon, who has used his knowledge to let the scoundrel artist die, so as to rescue (and perhaps marry) the wife, discovers that she is not grateful, cares nothing for him, and has in fact remarried. "Then," cries Ridgeon, "I have committed a purely disinterested murder!" The words we spoil or lose require footnotes at the bottom of the page, but footnotes don't go well behind the footlights.

Every trade or profession is entitled to its jargon. I use the word in its strict sense, which implies no disparagement. A proper, decent jargon consists of the words or applications of words that a trade has developed for clear and rapid communication. Sailors, carpenters, soldiers, priests, lawyers, air pilots are entitled to jargon and add to it as needed. The jargon of the old crafts is so expressive that a good deal of it has got into the common tongue, sometimes with mistaken meanings. In ordinary prose, *leeway, by and large, to back and fill, to go by the board* (*not* board*s*), *an anchor to windward* are borrowings from the sea, taken over for figurative use.

The newer professions, influenced by science and journalism, have produced, on the whole, poor jargons. They have been seduced into the manufacture of bad Greek and Latin compounds or equally pretentious English, deplorably vague. Hence it would not occur to a modern writer conscious of style

*This seems to be an allusion to Wordsworth's poem about the leech-gatherer, "Resolution and Independence." (Ed.)

to borrow from the chit-chat of sociologists or the asides of educators. Far better to echo the oculist with *20-20 vision* or the accountant with *bottom line*. One is at least in the realm of the tangible and straightforward.

In the new specialties one finds also a pseudo jargon, that is, ways of speech not required by special facts, tools, or actions, but used on the contrary to avoid the definite and particular. The pseudo jargon of these experts, including businessmen, seems to be the real jargon of the public-relations crew. It has the same smell. Thus preachers and social workers no longer tell you something: they share it with you. And when you reply, they are likely to say, "Do I hear you saying . . . this or that?" They don't often hear me; I avoid talking with them; that is, am not available for contacting—in short, I refuse to interface.

Nothing illustrates so well the degree of barbarism we have attained than the diction with which people presumably educated and even "intellectual" conduct their daily affairs. A young friend of mine who is a writer submitted his first book to a university press that I suggested. He received this reply: "I am pleased to acknowledge receipt of your manuscript. Upon initial review of this material, you will be contacted further."

Now although many people are unaware of the fact, "I am pleased" is not a nice expression. It does not mean "I am glad," (or happy), but "it pleases me"—it is the formula of royalty condescending to a subject. (Remember that a judge serves "during her majesty's pleasure.")

But let this pass, since the meaning has now been blurred. The rest of the letter is bad enough. "Upon initial review" is silly-pompous: whatever the upshot is, it will come *after*, not *upon*. "Initial," which only means *first*, makes one ask: how many times do they plan to confer? And *review* is premature. Reviews only come after publication. Here it is a stuffy word for *reading*. Next, what are they about to read? Not "this material"; he did not submit six yards of Harris tweed, but a book, a manuscript, as was shrewdly perceived in the first line of the letter.

As for "you will be contacted further," it is an improbable tale on the face of it. The author lives hundreds of miles away and contact is out of the question—think of contact sports, which are rightly named. It follows that *further* is foolish too. The sentence as a whole suggests spy fiction rather than civilized correspondence; it ought to read: "we shall write again," or: "you will hear from us."

"Plain English"—everybody loves it, wants it, demands it—from the other fellow. But the commodity is scarce. That same "everybody" stocks and supplies all sorts of fancy goods that aren't plain at all, while also making fun of those tradesmen whose line is said to be notorious for elaborate and murky effects—bureaucrats, journalists, academics, lawyers. Not long ago, in an effort to protect consumers, the state of New York passed a law requiring plain English in certain types of leases and contracts: no more legalese!

The move is surely discriminatory: why not prohibit the other *-ese* idioms used in bureaus, newspapers, and the foggy bottom of education, to say nothing of the latest obscurantists, the literary critics? Of the lot, I would muzzle the lawyers last. For much of what is derided as legalese is in fact indispensable. Although *The New Yorker* quotes derisively "the legal mind at work," we need that mind and its traditional forms of expression if we are to forestall bad faith and keep down vicious conflicts.

Gowers made the point long ago in *The ABC of Plain Words*. If a contract or regulation is not worded in such a way as to separate unmistakably what is agreed upon from what is excluded, the parties will quarrel and one or other of them may seize on a comma to take an unfair advantage. Gowers' example had to do with the "wiping rags" to be supplied to the government. What *is* a wiping rag? Unless it is defined with painful accuracy in six or eight lines, any odds and ends will qualify. The aim of language here is not elegance or charm or immediate comprehension, it is cast-iron denotation that will resist being pulled about.

In situations where no contesting is to be feared, a single fit word will do—you ask a friend in another city to "get you a car" for use during your visit. You needn't specify further, relying on his judgment and knowledge of your intentions. But in a general directive to subordinates, "get" must first be formalized into "obtain" and this in turn expanded into: "and secure the free use of, by hiring, renting, leasing, or borrowing." The words offer happy suggestions and exclude buying and stealing.

Thus "plain English" for legal use, as for medical and scientific description, is plain in a different way from that of ordinary exposition. A state constitution, the by-laws of a club, dare not be as smooth as the Gettysburg Address. Each is appropriate to its occasion. There is bad legal writing, of course, and some very bad scientific writing, but their badness does not consist in the apparent hair-splitting and redundancy that people like to laugh at; it consists in mindless muddle, in rank ambiguity, in tortuous syntax. These faults are the same everywhere.

EXERCISE IN DISCRETION

To exercise what? Why, Discretion, of course. The words below deserve Everyman's second thoughts. The exercise is to be followed week by week without letup until the incriminated words have been worked out of the poisoned system, the vocabulary swept clean.

That is the first recommended phase. A second, marking gymnastic progress, consists in adding one word a day to each list. It is cheating to add the kind of word due on Tuesday to the Friday list. This prohibition may make life hard, but the further strain will keep the critical organ in shape.

Monsters To Keep At Bay

prioritize

thinsulate

groceteria

infopreneurs

Danscompany (dancers)

televangelist

self-destruct

leisurize

atrium (*court*)

Hydramatic

Artforum (*a magazine*)

Midlantic

Flexble (*a bus*)

splanch (*split level
ranch*)

Americathon (*nation-wide
program*)

rustsicles (*on* Titanic *hull*)

claymation (*sculpture*)

Proximology (*title of a ballet*)

Ebonics (*Black English
for schools*)

tristimulus (*theory of color*)

homophobia (*fear of
homosexuals*)

Noirathon (*French
film festival*)

deaccession (*sell a
museum holding*)

Texaschusetts (*geological
underpinning*)

Mareps (*mariner
reports = sea news from
the Weather Bureau*)

audioanimatronic
(*Mickey Mouse
at Disneyland*)

TUESDAY
Ignorance To Remove

meld (*not: merge or
blend*)

volatile (*what can fly or
evaporate*)

masterful (*not: masterly—
e.g. work*)

avid (*only what can be
hungered for*)

coalesce (*only what can
flow together*)

immodest (*not: conceited*)

(lend) credence (*not:
make believable*)

schizophrenia (*not: split
personality*)

torturous (*no such word*)

ignite (*only what can burn*)

burgeoning (*not: blooming or
widespread*)

to a degree (*not: in part*)

litany (*not: a list*)

embattled (*not: besieged or
beset*)

inchoate (*not: incoherent*)

ambivalent (*not: ambiguous*)

sensuous (*not: sensual,
voluptuous*)

WEDNESDAY
Jargon To Eliminate

catalyst
scenario
quantum leap
empathy
low key
strategy
paradigm
mundane
parameter
acidic
-itis
facility (*not: a building*)
anathema (*not: he was an*)

metaphor (*only for metaphors*)
one on one (*only in basketball*)
geriatric (*only for care of the old*)
pre-emptive (*forestall, not: prevent*)
treasure trove (*a lucky find*)
dichotomy (*separation, division*)
peer (*= fellow, mate, equal*)
dilemma (*predicament*)
unquote
profile (*only faces and mountains*)

THURSDAY
Voguery To Eschew

creative
thrust
gender (*not: sex*)
gap
perception
abrasive
major
in depth
problem (*try: difficulty*)
as of (*try: on, at, when*)
meet with
dialogue
agonizing
process
legendary
impact
ALAS (Automated Library Acquisition System, alas!)

sensitive (*only skin, plant, soul*)
address (*only envelopes and audiences*)
testament (*only last will and*)
unveil (*only physical things*)
dimension (*only the measurable*)
overall
meaningful
concept (*try: idea, scheme, plan, notion*)
visit with
in terms of
decision-making (*decide*)
hopefully
no comment (*not an answer to a question*)
political retirement/oblivion

79

Question Beggers To Reject

romantic (He is . . .)

realistic (I am . . .)

medieval (notion)

reactionary (opinion)

socialistic ⎫
communistic ⎬ (*"istic" is the begging element*)
modernistic ⎭

conventional (*for: traditional—method, army, furniture*)

puritanical (attitude)

conservative (estimate)

affordable (*for: low-priced*)

radical (*in praise or blame*)

fascist ⎫ (*to denounce,*
liberal ⎭ *not describe*)

arguable (*for: doubtful*)

scientific ⎫
unscientific ⎭ (*who says so?*)

Verbs To Turn Right Side Out

It rankled them badly

This door is alarmed

The company must divest

She was convinced to buy

The manager was tasked with finding new answers

The party exited their limousines

This translates to $10

Joy percolates to a healthy glow

The pact culminates a long parley

It boggles the mind

I chose to sit tight and defend

That's a remark likely to inflame

The committee is comprised of five women and two men

It's easy to get large fees if you consult

This sampler dates to my great grandmother's time

Our effort should be to reconcile and start afresh

SUNDAY
Rest and Contemplate the Good

wind chill
backlash
teenager
grid lock
data bank
junk bonds
jet engine (jet lag, jet set)
shopping mall
stretch limousine
networking
space walk (space law)

radwaste
shuttle (*plane or space craft*)
zipper
creme de mink (*fur*)
lint trap
brisker (*electric food warmer*)
tax shelter
sun screen (*facial cream*)
tot lot (*park playground for infants designed, and term coined, by the late Arthur Shurcliff*)

False Friends

A Copy Editor's Anthology

In the spring of 1985, I published a brief article entitled "Behind the Blue Pencil—Censorship or Creeping Creativity?" It described the current practices of copy editors, the persons—many of them young—who are employed by publishers of books and magazines to prepare manuscripts for the printer. Once upon a time their role was to make the text clear and reasonably uniform in its use of capitals, punctuation, and the like. If thoughtful and well educated, they could also serve the author and the publisher by catching slips of the pen or the mind and by querying doubtful statements of fact. All writers have had cause to be grateful to his or her alert copy editor.

But latterly, most of these helpful people have taken it upon themselves to be critics, rewriters, virtual co-authors. They cross out phrasing they do not like, substitute adjectives, shorten, lengthen, recast, add names and facts, and generally have a field day in the author's pages. The gentler editors produce these unsolicited improvements on little slips of gummed paper which are attached to the margin of the script. They are called flags. After its acceptance and before it goes to the printer, the manuscript is returned to the author all flags flying—perhaps 300 of them in a work of average length. At other times an arrogant editor will enter his or her "suggestions" direct in the text, where they mingle confusingly with the author's own previous alterations. In any event, the author faces the task of re-reading, deciding, justifying and, in the flagless mutilation, erasing and restoring his own words.

My article gave examples of the hardship entailed for the author, of the harm done to style by gratuitous "homogenizing," and of the frequent errors blithely introduced by the ill-informed among copy editors. This exposé struck a responsive chord. The piece was quickly reprinted in four journals concerned with writing and I received many letters, some from aggrieved copy editors, but most from bruised authors still nursing their wounds. It is from the latter's proffered testimony that I have culled the examples that follow. They represent one more menace to good writing and, in their detail, they show how not to think and write. The damage inflicted is due to the author's compliance, conscious or not. If he is young and it is his first book that is bleeding on that surgical table, the fear of offending his publisher causes the submissiveness. If more experienced, the writer may be careless, weary, or insidiously swayed into the belief that one wording is as good as another. By firing so many shots, the sniper is felt to have earned the reward of acquiescence. In either case, individual style and free utterance are impaired.

What is more, usage is as it were being manufactured by the incompetent. It is a paradox that when language at large is being roughly treated by the heedless, a set of rigid notions and worthless rules are being enforced by the unliterary and ill educated. Thus split infinitives (or what are wrongly thought to be infinitives), sentences ending with a preposition, paragraphs beginning with *And* or *But*, capitals for titles of persons, hyphens that make compounds easy to read—all these are objects of copy-editor persecution. There is, besides, the perpetual "*which* hunt," whereby prose is studded with *that*'s regardless of sound or sense. At the same time, the common French phrases often misspelled by authors—*bête noire, crime passionnel* and the like—as well as the accents required on others, get by uncorrected. As for current jargon and vulgarisms, they regularly fail to prompt the blue pencil, being perhaps the copy editor's native tongue.

The sampling that follows will be seen to support the charges cited above and will illustrate *a contrario* some happy turns of phrase and nuances of thought.

Author's wording	Copy-editor's alteration
extruded	extracted
fathers	forebears
tried	strove
Muslim	muslin
Chichén Itzá	Chicken itzá
brandy	decaffeinated tea
jetsam	flotsam
debatable	unimpressive
postman	postal service employee
powers that be	powers that are in charge

The last two examples point to the most conspicuous of copy editors' defects—deafness to rhythm. One well-known columnist, who also writes novels and travel books, reports that in an article that began in a proper rhythmic way with the words: "My cook Gloria," his editor demanded that it be recast into: "Gloria Cervantes, my Mexican-American cook." A writer on philosophical subjects, discussing Pascal's views on faith, wound up with a summary of his author's advice to honest skeptics:

"Hear Masses, take holy water, and your doubts will fade." Imagine the writer's feelings on seeing in the printed article:

" 'Hear Masses, take holy water, and your doubts will fade,' Pascal advised."

Proper names trigger in editors the strongest urge to interfere without reason or knowledge. In a scholarly work on the law, the great eighteenth-century jurist Lord Mansfield was mentioned. He got by once with his correct title; the next time he became *Lord William* Mansfield, which made him not an earl at all, but the younger son of a peer enjoying only the courtesy title "Lord." In an encyclopedia entry of mine, where Agassiz was cited as a teacher of William James, the proof came back with "Alexander Agassiz." Since Alexander was almost exactly James's age, he was not likely to be his teacher; he was the son of Louis Agassiz, the man intended. Now, nobody has heard of son Alexander, and Agassiz, a notable scientist, sufficed. But no, copy editors must tamper and teach—most often the wrong things.

Perhaps nervous fiddling becomes an uncontrollable habit when one earns one's bread by striking, slashing, changing. A novelist reports that in his dialogue a character referred to seeing a play with the Lunts heading the cast. The marginal suggestion was: "Wouldn't the Hunts be better?" Nor are authors when dead free of this tinker's curse: a critic who quoted Somerset Maugham found the passage bespangled with marks in blue and red (one for words, the other for punctuation). And since, as everybody knows, Shakespeare was a criminally careless writer, why not help him out? For a recent work, an author's well-educated main editor had suggested an apt motto from *Hamlet*:

> Those friends thou hast in their adoption tried,
> Grapple them unto thy soul with hoops of steel.

In the finished book (40,000 copies printed) the second line appears as:

> Grapple them to the soul . . .

The ignorance that supposes *flotsam* and *jetsam* to be interchangeable has moments of self-awareness which may lead to "research." When an experienced writer characterized an Alpine resort by saying: "You can gambol all day and gamble all night," his copy scanner was troubled and telephoned him: "What is this *gamból*? I called up the Austrian Consulate but they couldn't help me."

At this point it is a mistake to laugh, as if the situation were one of those trifling things it is best to take in stride. For the same mixture of not knowing and not knowing where to look leads to the assumption that a piece of writing is made up anyhow, out of bits of pieces found in the *World Almanac* and the nearest foreign consulate. This belief permits the confident addition or substitution of ideas. A woman who has had notable success as a writer of children's books marked by an elegant simplicity of style was livid on discovering, after passing the proofs, that a whole (and commonplace) sentence had been inserted without a by-your-leave. Another writer, as much alive to social nuances as his copy reader, referred to "a responsible man of good breeding." This description was clearly undemocratic and sexually one-sided; it became: "a responsible person of good education," though in the historical context women *and* education were entirely irrelevant.

These are but small transgressions. Many an editor is determined to furnish thoughts out of her own stock to eke out the author's poor supply. A remarkable work by a jurist, published by a leading university press, came back to him in typescript with innumerable improvements of that sort. Where he had written: "Legal thinking, like the ocean, retains the heat of an idea longer than the atmosphere around it." The text now read: "Legal thinking retains the heat of an intellectual concept longer than the atmosphere around it, much as the ocean's temperature changes more slowly than the air's."

Fellow authors, take note! Avoid "ideas" and stick to "intellectual concepts"! And when you have said a thing once, and well, repeat it in clumsy duplicate. Your readers, poor souls, are helpless and docile and you can safely disregard them. But you will have placated your copy editors, whichever breed you may happen to find supervising your message: one kind will be soothed by your bumbling on, the other will recast your redundant sentence and write in the margin: "tighten up!"

A fair summing up of what goes on came to me from two mathematicians, well versed in writing for journals learned and popular. They detected in the script of their twenty-five-page essay the ravages of at least three editors. They proceeded, appropriately enough, to examine the data statistically. They found useful, and adopted with gratitude, 15 per cent of the changes. They swallowed, for the sake of peace, 10 per cent more, which were harmless though unnecessary. Another set they yielded to, because of "apparently rigid house rules." Adding in typographical errors, the total accepted was 40 per cent of the markings.

That left 60 per cent, which they also classified under: (1) insensitivity to style; (2) misunderstanding of meaning or intention; (3) misunderstanding of the mathematics itself. These figures do not mean that only 60 per cent of the alterations were wrong or offensive; for in the 40 per cent that the authors accepted or gave in to were 10 per cent of unnecessary ones and 15 per cent of typos and "rigidities." The useful contribution of three editors therefore amounted to perhaps 20 to 22 per cent of the multicolored changes.

This ratio is not inconsiderable and deserves full credit. No writer would do anything but bless and kiss his or her copy editor if that often anonymous deity caught all the typos, blind misspellings, fugitive commas, and verbal lapses. These very things are what led to the creation of the role, which was faithfully played within constitutional limits for many years. In a few firms the old practice subsists. Elsewhere, the question arises whether the evident usefulness of editing is not bought at too high a price. The price is paid in two forms. One is the mindless anarchy exemplified in the letters from correspondents that I have drawn on here—error, confusion, arrogance, and coercion, all doing damage to style and intellectual independence.

The other cost is waste of time. On this, too, the authors who confided their grievances were eloquent: "at the cost of ten hours of our joint time," wrote the mathematicians, "we, etc." Another writes: "This spring I worked for six weeks, undoing. . . ." Again, "As I write at least 80 per cent of the contents of the Newsletter, I am sorely beset by the changes which, etc. . . ." And so it goes: "He had me saying things that just were not so, and I had therefore to. . . ."/ "changed every *which* to *that* unless a comma preceded, and so. . . ."/ "It would have taken me the better part of two days simply to undo the damage. I sent it back to the publisher and told him to send me a clean draft."

This last, authoritative measure is not one that everybody can take. In *authority*, the word *author* has steadily shrunk. Unless he or she is well-known and profitable, the publisher's answer to being "told" anything may be equally masterful—or shuffling. It is remarkable to what extent nowadays the head of a firm is reluctant to give orders, much more to reprove. It is not that copy editors are scarce, might flounce out, and be hard to replace. But they have the same rights as other employees not to be fired without cause, and how in the present state of affairs could it be a cause that a well-written article or book had been garbled fore and aft and the writer compelled to rescue his meaning and style by hours of furious drudgery? Why, even the modern critics from France and from Yale will tell you that there is no reason to suppose the author knows his meaning better than anybody else.

The Naïveté of Spelling Reform

Among the letters I receive from strangers, I am favored from time to time with a summons to help do something about English spelling. Since I favor clarity in writing, why not cut out the underbrush and make words stand out clear and plain by spelling them the way they are pronounced? In a recent such missive, the opening challenge was:

"What is lost if we spell the names of the documents differently?—DeKLuREXuN uv iNDIPeNDuNS, KaNSTiTuXuN —the sounds are the same, the meanings are the same, the ideas are the same. Only the *unnecessarily complicated* spelling is changed. During a transition phase, *interlinear* versions will be handy."

The whole case is put in these few lines, though the writer adds that by converting foreign languages to the same system, teaching and learning them would be much simplified. That the example offered for French reads DEKLARASYO Da-DEPODOS does not seem to faze the advocate of simplicity and uniformity.

But to argue about a new system—one among many proposed during the last two hundred years—is to jump ahead of the real question. It will be time to choose the best way to spell after one has weighed the consequences of the change. (The same applies also to the schemes proposed, though less frequently, for making musical notation "easier.")

Most advocates of spelling reform are candid enough to say that their proposal, whichever it may be, is a "fundamental," a "radical" transformation; otherwise it would not be "rational." And it is here that the first consideration enters: What will happen if all at once we make obsolete and unreadable the forms in which the sifted legacy of the past is expressed, the culture embodied in words or notes and reproduced through print? The answer is simple: in one generation all the knowledge and beauty amassed in three thousand years will become a blank. I have no doubt that geniuses would continue to be born, some of whom might even strike out more freely in directions now unimagined, but the time would be long before a comparable treasure would collect, and the interim would be bleak. There is plenty of oblivion and careless rejection as it is. And anybody who thinks that "interlinear versions" and transliteration into the new system would take place and preserve "all that is really good" knows nothing about economics or publishing. The loss would be immense and absolute.

Such is the first, *general* objection to spelling reform, better named spelling revolution. The *particular* objection is, if possible, even more potent. The tinkers with spelling agree on one point; they all say: "make it phonetic—let us spell as we pronounce." Very nice, but *whose* pronunciation? I listen daily to the local weather bureau, where I have singled out by ear six announcers, of whom one is a woman and one almost certainly a black—a man with a splendid deep voice. The six pronounce the same words differently: the black drops the g in -*ing* like a British aristocrat; the young woman says *an'*, not *and*. Some of the others say *humi-ity*, also without a *d*. There is *tempra-cher* and *temperchoor*; *Tyusday and Toosday*; the word *center* occurs as *cent'er* and as *cennt-ter* (a New Yorkism); the number 20 is spoken as *twanny*, *twenny*, and *twennt-ty*. This is but a sampling of the wide diversity of sounds actually uttered to signify common words.

If spelling is to be truly phonetic, these variations must lead to multiple forms of the same word. And they are only the beginning. For there are other types of diversity. We must reckon with regional, class, and ethnic differences. Educated Boston speaks of *lawr-and-awduh* and the *cawt house*, whereas

Ohio says *law-anorderr* and the *corrthouse*. It also says *Hairy* for *Harry* and *vahrious* for *various*. Many Texans and Californians say *pin* for *pen* and vice versa, and treat these vowels the same way in other words. The South, from Georgia to Texas, shapes its consonants and drags its vowels so that no single system can arise within the region, much less within the larger area that includes it. A student last summer told me he was "drivin' to Balldimer in a Ponniac"; a colleague in Louisiana stops at the "bayunk" on his way to "wuh-urk."

Besides this daunting pluralism, we must remember that the English language does not belong to the United States alone, or to North America. The British Isles, Australia and New Zealand (locally called New Zillund), the subcontinent of India, many islands in the seven seas, large parts of Africa, and thousands of Europeans, Asians, and Latin Americans have learned English and modified its utterance in countless ways. Some cannot say *th*, others invert *v* and *w*, while the sounds of *r*, *l*, *b*, and *d*, and the vowels vary indefinitely. What makes them all "speak English" is the central, conventional spelling of the words that they voice as they please or as they can.

Two things follow. If each individual spells the way he speaks, or thinks he speaks, old chaos returns and destroys ready communication in writing. If some sort of regional phonetic spelling is adopted—one for India, one for Britain, one for Texas—that spelling becomes a convention and therefore "inaccurate" and "difficult," not only for inhabitants of other regions, but also for every individual in any region, except the most prissy and fussy speakers.

Nor is this all. The reformers' supposedly strong argument—automatic knowledge of how to spell and hence ease of teaching, reading, and writing—is pure fantasy. For ease of reading and teaching, the different look of words that sound alike is important: *rain, reign,* and *rein* tell us instantly the idea we should form. Spell them all *rane* and the three meanings and associations are blurred. The truth is that words in modern languages have become in part ideographic—pictures of sense. This fact is what led to the massive disaster of the look-and-say method of teaching reading: it expected that these "pictures" could be learned in infancy, each by itself, without the preliminary aid of the alphabetic sounds. The error shows that phonics are the only workable starting point. But in due course, for adults, the "misspelling" from the phonetic point of view turns into an invaluable time- and effort-saver.

Now consider the effect of spell-as-you-speak on teaching. To begin with, a *nearly* adequate phonetic system—one matching the sounds we speak—would require not twenty-six letters but forty-three. This addition means added difficulty for the child starting school. And as to phonetic detail, it is a question how far a child—indeed, any person—is aware of how he does pronounce. That unconsciousness is shown in the quite different spellings by the same hand in letters written 300 years ago, before spelling was set. This irregularity in turn reminds us that any speaker pronounces the same words differently in successive sentences: "I gave 'em to 'im"—"No! not *them*; yes, to *him*!" Do you say *No* or *Naw*? Don't you in fact say both? I do.

There is, in short, no likelihood of phonetic accuracy or fixity in any spelling scheme whatever. Even if one were devised and agreed upon by the scattered millions of English speakers all over the globe, it could not last in its purity very long. Pronunciation shifts in time as well as in space, like everything else. In Dr. Johnson's day, people drank *tay* out of *chainey coops*, but he preferred *poonch*. We should be thankful that they spelled ("absurdly") *tea, china,* and *cups,* which we can still decipher.

Don't think that's the end. The components of teaching and reading are not done with in the first grade. To grasp meanings and use appropriately an increasing vocabulary requires a knowledge of connections. In the present system, the links of meaning between words are marked through letters even when the sounds change. We say *layber, luhborius,* and *labra-*

tory, but through reading we learn them as variations on the root *labor*. English is especially rich in words whose derivatives or compounds displace the stress accent. Get rid of conventional spelling and these connections disappear; children will have to be taught that the state of Maryland has something to do with *land* and with *Mary*; the forty-three symbols won't tell him at sight—and he will get another shock when he hears some of the natives call it *Murlin*.

As to foreigners who want to learn English, the obstacle of a new and strange alphabet will not contribute to "ease." Unless their own countries have also adopted it, it will be like the barrier of the Russian or Greek letters now; whereas the Roman alphabet in use today and the vocabularies of the Western languages offer hundreds of words so similar in spelling that they are understood at sight. But the sounds given to these cognates are also *similar* and not the same. So a new phonetic alphabet will not resemble those pieces of clothing advertised as "one size fits all." (French, incidentally, is spelled in ways much more arbitrary, difficult, even perverse, than English; and the irrationality is compounded by the anarchical practice of *liaisons* between words. The language, in short, could support the simplification thesis far better than English.)

Even supposing the alphabet hurdle taken in stride by the foreign learner, the ideographic problem will recur: in his bilingual dictionary all the homophones will need special differentiation: pale (a light tint of any color)/ pale (a small container)/pale (a district around a city). And so for dozens of pairs or triplets. A foreigner whose own language had kept the advantage of differentiation through varied spellings might well exclaim, "Why don't those English peoples go in for a bit of spelling reform!'

This imagined complaint points to the fatal trait of utopian reformers in general: they naively believe that they will still have the advantages of the old system after they have discarded it for the new. Because these blessings are familiar they seem somehow "given," indestructible. Or, more naive still, the reformers do not even perceive that anything now in use has advantages. They lack equally observation and imagination.

Must we then continue to suffer *believe* and *receive*, *bow*, *bow*, and *bough*, while the foreigner struggles with *though* and *tough*, *through*, *slough*, and *slough*? On the whole, yes. These well-publicized difficulties are preferable to the many more that would arise from attempts at a rational uniformity, especially if based on the false idea that pronunciation is the way to it. In practice, many of the difficulties of spelling are odd enough to strike the learner's memory in a permanent way. They break up the monotony of word drill and prepare for the far greater irregularities of meaning and idiom, which occur in all languages and which are the very means of flexibility and subtlety in a well-developed tongue.

Now, if somebody wants to trim a word here and there—make it *beleeve* and *receeve*—I would regret it but not object violently. It would leave our past in print still readable. Nobody is put off by finding *honour* where one expects *honor*; or, in older books, *publick*, which we have slimmed down to *public*. It would be good if the *e* were regularly left out of *likeable*, *saleable*, *mileage*, and other words where it plays no role. Nor is there any harm in preferring *traveler* with one *l* and *advisor* with *er*. But changes of this sort must come by the tacit and gradual consent of *writers*—not by edict from editors or compilers of handbooks, who never look ahead. How far, for example, would the adoption of *receeve* carry us? Would we feel the need of *receet* for *receipt*? And if so, shall we miss the link between *receipt* and *recipe* and *reception*? As soon as one tampers, it implies—or seems to imply—a principle; and principles have an awkward way of clashing with their neighbors. Etymology is a principle, and here it conflicts with "ease" and "logic."

Another principle is consistency: with *receeve* and *receet* in hand, won't someone want to convert *deceit* and *conceit*, which have lost the *p* of *receipt* but are parallel forms, with *deception* and *conception* in the offing. The likely answer is that one writer will want to "fix" one thing (by *un*fixing it); another will change another; together they will only further confuse what is already irregular. That irregularity is not arbitrary but historical, and on that account has been absorbed and accepted; it is in all the dictionaries, in all the books, in all the minds most concerned. To change any part of it consciously *will* be an arbitrary act, and if it is not followed semiconsciously by others, it will not be historical but eccentric. But the naive spelling reformer sets out to *remove* eccentricity. If his efforts lead to the puzzles I have pointed out, his must remain a DeKLuREXuN uv iNDiPeNDuNS without any signers or followers.

Basic English: Whose Pidgin Is It?

Basic English is like the Mona Lisa: any serious consideration of its merits is disturbed by the wish to forget both the weight of convention and the lure of rebellious dissent. It does not help one to make up one's mind about Basic English that this limited language is addressed to foreigners in the hope of making their entry into the English-speaking world easier. The question always remains whether ready communication depends on the extent and difficulty of a vocabulary or on something else not so readily controlled.

In his new version of Plato's *Republic* the well-known scholar and critic I. A. Richards adopts the former hypothesis, without, however, adhering strictly to Basic English. He uses more verbs than the list allows and thus avoids the "noun plague" that characterizes Basic. As he told readers of *The Nation* in the issue of March 28* he wants to make Plato's debate on government accessible to the widest possible circle of readers—readers who he thinks are always alienated by the leisurely pace and poetic flourishes of the original and its translations. He has therefore cut, condensed, and retranslated with an eye to simplicity.

The result does not strike me as fulfilling his intention. Setting aside objections of detail, I am more than ever convinced by this new version that the ease with which a presumed lowbrow will take to a classic does not depend wholly or even mainly on forms of speech. It depends, rather, on the familiarity or unfamiliarity of the ideas and their sequence. A great pop-

*1942 (Ed.)

99

ular writer—say, Dickens or Conan Doyle—can use big words and involved constructions and still be widely understood, because what these point to is relatively commonplace. A difficult writer—say, Henry James in *The Ambassadors*—can use short words and short sentences and still give the impression of complexity and obscurity, because his substance is new and strange. So with Plato, the way of arguing—I might even say the need to argue—can hardly be made attractive to those who do not already feel some liking for the enterprise and are not willing to put some effort into following its course.

I agree, to be sure, with Mr. Richards's rule that we should translate the classics into our own contemporary speech and not into some artificial and would-be archaic idiom. In the preface of Samuel Butler's version of Homer, the translator gave the definitive reason for this choice: "Nothing is readable, for long, which affects any other diction than that of the age in which it is written."

This is a less pretentious reason than that which Mr. Richards gives in his introduction to *The Republic*, for Mr. Richards's mind is aglow with pedagogical earnestness. He believes that we should all read Plato for the sake of democracy. It is not clear to me how Plato's Spartan regime with class barriers and intellectual censorship is going to help keep up our spirits; and on general principles I suspect the elevation of any single book to the rank of scripture. In any case, Plato does *not* contain all that matters in political theory. The Greeks have *not* said the last word on any subject, however much we may admire what they did say. The notion of the last word is absurd, at least until after the Last Trump.

The same strained eagerness vitiates Mr. Richards's other publication, *How to Read a Page*, which is meant to accompany *The Republic*. By discussing the ambiguities of some hundred important words this manual intends to correct Professor Adler's *How to Read a Book* and to take precedence over Professor Buchanan's discipline of the Hundred Great

Books. It does not in fact accomplish either of these tasks, being a hodge-podge of semantics, propaganda for Basic, literary criticism, political theory, and theology. Though patronizing in spots and offensively cute in others, the work bears little relation to the description given on the jacket, "A Course in Efficient Reading." It is itself extremely difficult to read, and at best it only establishes the fact that prose needs as much interpreting as poetry.

Mr. Richards's own prose certainly needs it. One would guess that the text had been dictated if this supposition did not entail the further one that Mr. Richards had no ear. How else account for a sentence like "This illustrates well a point in these notes of very great importance"? That is unfortunately a fair sample. On one page Mr. Richards preaches precision in the use of words; on another he argues that it is pedantry to insist on correct usage, because context gives meaning to most uses and even misuses. In this theoretical contradiction Mr. Richards follows the practice of the imprecise. He is addicted to the usually meaningless connective "in terms of"; he will not distinguish between "specific" and "particular" any more than between "shall" and "will"; and his mismanagement of pronouns is such as frequently to obscure all meaning. Indeed, his book directs attention not so much to the value of semantics and Basic for good reading as to the still more elementary maxim that "easy writing makes damned hard reading." Correct emphasis, placement, rhythm, and inner relations—in short, the old problems of prose that "pedants" still worry about—do not occupy Mr. Richards sufficiently. He evades these difficulties in part by proposing a new set of seven distinct quotation marks, composed of small letters, which he himself uses with a liberality that seems to say again, "the reader will do the work."

There would be much to add about the philosophic and social implications of Mr. Richards's present failure if it were viewed in the light of the many services to literature he has previously rendered; but speaking of pedantry, who is this Francis of Verulam who supplies a number of mottoes to Mr. Richards's chapters? Isn't "Bacon" Basic?

In a speech at Harvard in 1943, Winston Churchill referred to Basic English as "a carefully wrought plan for . . . transactions of practical business and interchange of ideas . . . a medium of understanding to many races, and an aid to the building of a new structure for preserving peace." Those sanguine words have not been borne out by experience. Understanding among peoples and the exchange of ideas require more than a common tongue, as every national or family dispute readily shows. And Basic English, however wrought, is peculiarly unable to help, because its very method denies the importance of shades of meaning. The roster of 850 words, of which 600 are nouns and only eighteen verbs, enables the speaker not so much to express what is on his mind as to say only what his vocabulary allows.

Here, from the *Handbook of Basic English* (1945), is how one has to put the thought "We often hear it said of someone . . .": "This opinion of someone is frequently given to us." In the Gettysburg Address we read: "a new nation, conceived in liberty (Basic: designed to be free) and dedicated to the proposition (and given to the theory) that all men are created equal (are to their Maker equal). The differences are not as slight as Basic Englishers would maintain; they are of the size that produces the bitterest quarrels. To conceive in liberty is not the same as to design for freedom; to be dedicated to a proposition is not to be "given to a theory," which implies a mental crotchet; and being created equal does not ensure our Maker's thinking that we have remained so. Of such deviations in wording is religious or political persecution born.

One may object that Basic English was never meant to do more than assist business dealings and shipboard romance. Perhaps not, but the Churchillian faith in a made-up tongue is tenacious, and as it rests on a fallacy about language the scheme deserves a brief scrutiny. Have you ever read *Hamlet* in Esperanto? No, well, after the first few moments of uncontrollable hilarity, because the familiar words sound as if travestied by a clever comedian, one settles down like a fair-minded adult to follow the irresistible plot and powerful stream of idea and emotion. But to one's surprise, though the plot is not obscured, no ideas and emotions arise from it; they are not there.

Or, to be exact, they are there only when one happens to remember the original English. The new words do not vibrate; they fall on the mind like lead coins. Why is this? Surely any combination of syllables that can be spoken must possess some resonance, and Esperanto, which draws its roots from the Romance languages, sounds pleasing enough. All this is true; what the discourse lacks altogether is a set of associations; the words and groups of words have never been charged with power through proverbs, through historic declarations, through great works of art, through talk at the dinner table.

This last source of power might indeed come into existence, but then the Esperanto family would shortly find gaps and obstacles in the vocabulary and proceed to deal with them. Impatient at roundaboutnesses they would take short-cuts, create idioms, begin to make and speak *a language*. At that point it will cease to be Esperanto and its capability as an international medium of communication will disappear. There will be need of a new scheme, an Esperantissimo, to get back to the position of neutral tongue intended by the maker—by the maker of any artificial language.

"Artificial language" is in fact a contradiction in terms, just as Basic English is a misnomer. Basic has the faintest relation to English, the feeblest possible "base" in it, namely 850 words *spelled* like English words but denatured by the rules— not English, scarcely human—to which they are subjected. Consider one general case: All verbs other than the licit eighteen are made by using nouns according to this rigid formula: "The man *moves* and the man *moved* are not permissible ... Equivalents for these expressions may be made by using with *moving* [from *move*, one of the 400 'nouns of things'] different forms of the word *be* [sic]: 'the man is moving' and 'the man was moving.' " To take the English (progressive) tense, which is the strangest to foreigners, as the single verb form for all Basic utterances seems almost perverse.

Besides this singularity, naming things outside the elite 400 also requires circumlocution. *Soup* is available, but *potato* is not. The gourmet, if ingenious, will resort to: "plant with thick brown cover that is bursting from the earth" and will use this businesslike modifier in front of *soup*; on hearing which, the waiter may well be surprised.

And worse than surprised, tongue-tied; for even if the foreigner has chosen a restaurant with the sign "Basic English Is Saying Here," no one, not even the *head* waiter, can keep in mind what may and may not be replied to the foreigner in Basic. I. A. Richards himself had to stray out of bounds. No English speaker can help breaking the 850-word barrier and spilling out whatever is on his mind. And all the while, this mutual hindrance to self-expression that is built into Basic refutes its claim to facilitate the exchange of ideas. All it can do is give a damaging start—and many bad habits—to the would-be learner of English. He would do far better to begin with an actual pidgin, say, the Melanesian, which at least was born naturally and which does work—or else buy Senhor Pedro Carolino's *Guide to the Conversation** and use "the little book that may be worth the acceptation of the studious persons, and especially of the Youth at which we dedicate him particularly." Pedro is by a good eighth of an inch closer to English than Plato in Basic.

*See p. 35. (Ed.)

After Fowler's Generation

Those who were at the threshold of a writing career when "Fowler" appeared in 1926 feel among themselves a common bond unlike any other. It is, for one thing, an all-sufficing bond, which implies much else. That is why "Fowler" is such a superb conversation piece. It has the advantage of being an author and a single book, an oracle and an orthodoxy, and yet it is free from the disadvantage of infallible art and the burden of a historic personality. One cannot be tiresome about "Fowler" as about Jane Austen; one may be devoted to him but there can be no question of any love chatter. Fowler is only a comrade, the kind of friend with whom it is a pleasure to dispute.

What then is "Fowler"? To my generation the *Dictionary of Modern English Usage* came as a counselor and teacher, but also as a touchstone for a certain type of mind; the work was a social and not only an intellectual landmark. The dour title did not promise all these things, but readers soon found themselves involved in party feeling and moral questions. In browsing through the book they came, for example, upon the heading SUPERIORITY and found this:

"Surprise a person of the class that is supposed to keep servants cleaning his own boots, and either he will go on with the job while he talks to you, as if it were the most natural thing in the world, or else he will explain that the bootboy or scullery-maid is ill and give you to understand that he is, despite appearances, superior to bootcleaning. If he takes the second course, you conclude that he is not superior to it; if the first, that perhaps he is. So it is with the various apologies (*to use an expressive colloquialism—if we may adopt the current slang—as the streetboys have it—in the vernacular phrase . . .*) to which recourse is had by writers who wish to safeguard their dignity and yet be vivacious, to combine comfort with elegance, to touch pitch and not be defiled."

Or again, Fowler's pupils found the term GENTEELISM explained and exemplified by a list of words such as: *anent, assist, domestic, edifice, endeavour, lady-dog, perspire, peruse, proceed,* which are genteel when substituted for *about, help, servant, building, try, bitch, sweat, read* and *go.* To us who had just been reading Henry James on the Question of Our Speech and Santayana on the death of the genteel tradition, Fowler made it apparent that diction and idiom and style— Usage, in short—embodied the same social attitudes that we reproved in literature, attitudes having deep roots in our emotional life, where they found themselves in harmony, perhaps, or in conflict, with our political convictions.

What made the reading and re-reading of Fowler necesary was that despite his firm views he was not an easily classifiable doctrinaire. He knew, and said, that he was a gentleman—see the article ENGLAND; and he never hesitated to brand as affectation and vulgarity the cheap elegancies and looseness of mind sometimes associated with the democratic outlook. Yet he shared that outlook, and one had to conclude that he was not a purist or a pedant. He was not in awe of his own classical and modern learning; he used it to make things clear, never to gain merit by imposing some awkward form of words congenial only to the retrospective sense.

In short, Fowler showed by his precepts and by his style what it could mean to take a reasoned view of the democratic citizen's duty toward language. It meant making an effort to be understood but also to seek the best; it meant forgetting ego but not distinction. To that extent Fowler's way was aristocratic. The word *usage* once conveyed the combined obligations—the social one of pleasing by simplicity and clarity and suitability of language; and the intellectual one of respect for tradition and reason through a conscious choice of the best forms.

There was great need at the time, and there is greater need now, for this kind of counsel particularized. Sixty years ago the "scientific" opponents of grammar and usage were just triumphing over what they considered the old superstitions and snobberies, and in their crusade were using the fallacious arguments of natural growth, irresistible change, and democratic freedom. The aim was to encourage rather than restrain the anarchy which is the unavoidable first fact in the use of language. In a word, they made their arbiter Use as against Usage.

Today, these scientists command the field and hurl anathemas at all dissenters from their simple doctrine. Today also, we have an acknowledged "problem of communication." I am not suggesting here a strict sequence of cause and effect; but the linguists' propaganda has contributed to the "problem." The neglect of the conventions of speech and the self-applauding indulgence in haphazard use certainly play a part in that hardening of the mind's ear which, when general, we term failure of communication. One has only to read the literature on the "communication arts" to see in that prose itself where one great difficulty lies.

A Fowler, then, is always needed because the anarchy is always with us—in the United States especially; for here the English language is subjected to an inordinate amount of distortion, blurring, and confusion. Foreign speakers and writers are numerous, and the false liberalism of *laisser faire* gives prompt authority to error and caprice. It is not, of course, any single violation of meaning or idiom, however frequent, that harms the common property of language. If frequent, the error becomes general—becomes the language—in the traditional way of change. What does harm, now and hereafter, is the loss of the feeling for words, the disappearance of any instinct and any preferences about their formation and combination. For this soon means the abolition of convenient devices for being brief, exact, and possibly agreeable.

The scientific students of language, who inveigh with so much unscientific passion against normative grammar and ideals of correctness, assert that all one can ask of a speaker or writer is that he be "effective"—specious counsel which begs the question and raises another: How to be effective when conventions break down? One might as well expect motorists to drive "effectively" without lights or traffic rules, scrambling to their destination anyhow.

In any civilized country, the countervailing force which keeps the headlong and haphazard traffic in words from wrecking much useful machinery is the speech and writing of the educated. It is the felicities and dangers of this speech that Fowler discussed under many heads suggestive of the conventions, from pronunciation to syntax. And it is their variety, subtlety, and strength that Fowler made vivid in his spiky essays full of horrors.

Since his day, which ended in the mid-thirties, a new generation has grown up to whom he is no longer a household word, and changes have taken place in the language that alter the status of words and constructions formerly on trial. For both reasons a revised edition of his work was desirable, if possible one that might take account of American usage. The attempt by Horwill to provide an American companion to Fowler a few years after the appearance of *Modern English Usage* was a ludicrous failure, owing chiefly to the author's lack of familiarity with current American speech and writing. A fresh attempt was made in 1957, this time by an American, to supply the want while bringing Fowler up to date. *A Dictionary of American-English Usage*, by Margaret Nicholson was explicitly based on Fowler and addressed modern readers on either side of the Atlantic with a professedly equal voice. But the result was a disappointment. No one, to be sure, expected that a second Fowler of American birth would be found who could interlard the original doctrine with comparably entertaining and memorable pieces of instruction and reproof. It took a very special talent—a kind of genius—to conceive and execute *Modern English Usage*; and the curious like myself who hunted down Fowler's other essays, on life and letters, discovered that when deprived of his great subject the Petronius of style was an awkward and uninteresting writer. Again, in the earlier *King's English*, written with his younger brother Francis, one finds the same good judgment and extensive knowledge as in H. W.'s *Modern Usage*, but none of the strength, ease, and imagination of the later work.

It was to be expected, then, that even a competent, judicious alteration of "Fowler" would dim its brilliance; yet there would be compensation in a suitable modernizing and Americanizing of the original. Unfortunately, competence and judiciousness did not preside over the revision Miss Nicholson offered us. Except for a very few short articles, such as the ones on *comprise* and *disinterested*, the new matter hardly touched on modern usage—American *or* English—but dwelt on details of interest to copy editors, matters of preferred spellings, the italicizing and punctuating of abbreviations, and other things which scarcely affect language and about which it is in fact impossible to indicate prevailing practice.

In such preoccupations, Fowler's reviser did and does indeed represent the contemporary American philosophy of style: concerned with mechanics and careless of substance, engrossed in technicalities and deficient in knowledge. She uses valuable space to define *half binding* and *half title* as if she were competing with Collins' *Authors' and Printers' Dictionary*, and she passes by the most obvious gaps created in Fowler by the lapse of time and the transatlantic shifting of the point of view. For instance, she reproduces his definition of *to a degree* without a word about its unfortunate reversal of meaning, and she takes up *extent* without mentioning the new *to an extent*, built on the analogy of the other.

One may in fact generalize and say that Miss Nicholson went about her work without any clear idea of Fowler's original intention, hence of what adapting that intention to American problems might mean. Collating the pair of texts for opportunities missed yields a distressing quantity of serious failures. For example: under -AL NOUNS, Fowler called *appraisal* "unfamiliar and doubtful to the common man." Miss Nicholson copies this without a murmur; but under *appraisal* itself, she terms it "standard U.S." Under *amour-propre* she again follows Fowler in giving its meaning as "vanity," and fails to mention a frequent use of it in a meaning akin to "self-respect." Under *Anthony*, she asserts that "in U.S. the *h* is often pronounced, especially in surnames." I would undertake to gather into one room all the American citizens who do *not* pronounce the *h*.

Still copying Fowler, she repeats his strictures on *betterment* and *foreword*, which are by now standard U.S., with meanings perceptibly different from "improvement" and "preface." It is no longer unusual for a book to have a foreword *and* a preface. Again, had Fowler lived and emigrated, he would not have run past *catalogue* without a word about the forms "cataloged" and "cataloging" which enchant the devotees of library science; and—supposing him to have kept his eyes and ears open as of yore—he would not have persisted in his belief that *artiste* is a useful word. Still less would he have dreamed that anyone in America ever refers to "dirty work at the cross*ways*." (Meredith's title, however, is still *Diana of the Crossways*, not *Crossway*; the new "Fowler" is not so carefully proofread as its ancestor.)

A few more illustrations will show the same lack of judgment. One of Fowler's great services to speech was his attack on the false adverbial forms in *-ly* after verbs of sensation or motion; but he surely would not have been content to point out that the true colloquial idiom for "I am ill" is "I feel bad"; he would have added that "I feel badly" is also usual in another sense. Since the purpose of the revision was to bring matters up to date, how account for Miss Nicholson's disparaging definition of *baroque*, which is actually in retrogression over Fowler's more generous ones, written sixty years ago? And in the same aesthetic vein, why no mention of the special U.S. meaning of *burlesque* in "burlesque show"? English readers may consult this mutilated Fowler in the belief that they can learn colloquial speech well enough to use it in novels. If so, they are riding for a fall: imagine using *bunk* to signify "anything done for mere show; insincere publication, nonsense;" as in, presumably: "Henry Ford said, 'History is an insincere publication.'"

Most regrettable among the recurrent errors is that of not catching up Fowler's insularities and antiquities. He deserved better than to be mangled just enough for show, creating the impression of a systematic review and leaving him with his worst faults left—as in CHINAMAN, ETC.: "The normal uses are: *A Chinaman* (rarely *Chinese*); three *Chinamen* (sometimes *Chinese*); 50,000 *Chinese* (sometimes *Chinamen*); the *Chinese* (rarely *Chinamen*)" . . . "Chinaman (-men)" is now as purely colloquial as "Jap," and as offensive. On a number of graver matters, too, such as FUSED PARTICIPLE, Fowler now calls for amendment. Again, dozens of his quoted examples date from the reign of Edward VII and contain words and proper names as mysterious as the handwriting on the wall: American readers will stop only a moment at *wharf* and *treacle*, but what are they to make of "will not crane at" and what to them is the King's Proctor?

Besides alteration and excision, the modern reader had a right to expect liberal additions, in the spirit of Fowler, upon the errors, doubts and confusions of the previous quarter century. *Disinterested*, on which the editor is sound but mild, suggests a number of others. Why do we hear nothing of the American use, abuse, or misuse of *absenteeism, basic, cohort, connive, skills, compulsive, epoch, essential, evaluation, drastic, major,* or of the return to a double *as* in "*As* much as I like him, I can't forgive him," or the use of *-wise* and *-conscious* as all-purpose tails to other words?

One more remark is in order about Miss Nicholson's work

as a cultural document: it demonstrates in its new portions the need for just such a dictionary as the original Fowler was. I spoke earlier of the single force counteracting the wear and tear of the language. That force is supposedly exerted by those who have done some studying and who come before the public as speakers and writers. Miss Nicholson was one of these and even more than this, since (as we were told) she was "formerly Head of the Publishing Department of Oxford University Press. In this capacity she worked with authors and Oxford editors in the revision and final editing of manuscripts accepted for publication." It is therefore doubly allowable to ask: How does she write?

A former guardian of forms, an arbiter of taste, perhaps a begetter of new felicities, she may have missed her aim as a lexicographer of usage, but surely she must be one of those on whom we can rely for exact diction and coherent utterance. Alas, alas! her writing plunges us into despair from the outset. In keeping with her mechanic habit of mind she begins by abbreviating the title of Fowler's classic to MEU, heading her Preface with a motto from him labeled in this barbaric way. Throughout the Preface, this pseudo-Chinese sage recurs, in alternation with her own misbegotten AEU, quite as if the affectionate initials O.E.D. (or GBS) licensed indiscriminate imitation.

The tone of that Preface, moreover, is patronizing under a pretense of admiration. Fowler is "provocative," and it appears that "many of us today, English and American, have neither the time nor the scholarship to follow through the fascinating but sometimes exasperating labyrinth. . . ." Moreover, Fowler is guilty of the "Socratic method of teaching by wrong examples [*sic*]." We are meant to think: here is a saner book for busier people. But it could be argued that the method of teaching by wrong examples has not been given up; the difference is that the wrong examples are now no longer quoted from others; they are the author's own. Scan the early pages:

. . . the absolute construction gives a heaviness of style; it is best used sparingly.

aestivate: summer sleeping as opposite of hibernate.

. . . except in prose of a really poetic type.

ambivalence: simultaneous attraction and repulsion to the same object or person.

amoral: not connected with morality.

apposite: appropriate (to), well put.

assonance: the careless repetition of sound in words or syllables [sole definition].

classified material: . . . "because of endangerment to national security."

federation, confederation, confederacy: there is no rigid distinction between the words.

fifth column: secret supporters of the enemy within the defense line.

corpus delicti: the basic facts necessary to the commission of a crime.

It is of course easier, though quite uncalled for in a book on usage, to define *haematoxylin* as is done on page 227; and perhaps a gift for definition is so rare that we should not expect it of editors who "work with authors on manuscripts accepted for publication." But we do expect correct information—since all it requires is looking up—as well as the ability to know how much description suffices to give a clear idea of the thing defined. The factual explanations in this garbled Fowler fail on all counts:

éclat: now used in English chiefly in the sense of universal acclamation.

chiaroscuro: in art, the employment of light and shade, omitting the colors [sole definition].

on the carpet: under discussion.

carte blanche: "white paper," hence, full discretionary power.

collage . . . Art: an assortment of fragments put together to make an artistic composition.

à[l']outrance: to the utmost, to death.

It is also a sign of the times that terms like these were included by Fowler solely for their easiest English pronunciation. He left to the ordinary dictionaries the task of explaining them unless some point of usage was connected with the word or phrase. This saved space, established coherence, and avoided the mock-encyclopedic effect toward which most American dictionaries strive. Meanwhile one weeps to see Fowler stripped and re-accoutered by an unskilled hand for ends which he would repudiate and which show him to his posterity of new readers in a deplorable travesty.

[It is gratifying to be able to add, thirty years after Miss Nicholson and sixty after Fowler, that a revised and suitably Americanized *Modern English Usage* did at last appear, under the wise and learned editorship of Sir Ernest Gowers.]

Dialogue in C-Sharp

The young man's politeness had ice in it—courtesy on the rocks. "Of course," he said, "if you insist, we have no choice but to change everything back the way you want it. It's too late for us to get another contributor and fill the gap that the withdrawal of your article would leave."

"But I'm not asking for anything very startling—only capitalization here and there, a few hyphens, and some wording that is perfectly normal and that I happen to prefer to yours."

" 'Capitalization here and there!' You don't realize that as head of copy-editing, I have a responsibility to my readers—the people who buy the books of this firm. They're very sharp about inconsistencies—and keen on the trend of modern writing—"

"What trend of modern writing?"

"The trend toward simpler, quicker, easier forms. The English language has got to be taken down, streamlined. Those capitals you want interrupt. They're an obstacle—"

"Do you mean to tell me—" here I started flipping through my page proofs— "that it makes reading easier to have the names of historical movements and parties without a capital? For instance: 'Zola was a naturalist;' 'the liberal prime minister, Gladstone'?"

"I do, and the *Chicago Manual of Style* agrees with me. We have to be consistent, which is why we—"

"You're consistent all right. You make Zola a naturalist, and then the reader comes upon: 'Darwin, the great naturalist.' You have the liberal prime minister, and later Edward

VII, who was also liberal—toward his mistresses. Why do you suppose capital letters were ever used? Why start sentences and paragraphs with capitals if they're an encumbrance? And let me add that your talk about ease of reading is a hoax, a fraud. Whenever you can, you run words together and make the reader puzzle out the result. See here: *antiintellectual* in one word. What is the point? What has been gained?"

"The *Chicago Manual*—"

"Never mind the *Manual*— it isn't holy scripture; I haven't joined a religious sect and taken an oath to be ruled by a book. My creed is that I put my name only to what I write; I write as I like; and I like hyphens—especially where they make reading easier. I don't much care for words that begin with *non-*, but if I use one I resent its being made unreadable by merging—*nonobjective, nonoperative.* All these *nonos* annoy me and in my published prose I say "No, no" to them, with a comma in between, if you please."

"Well, if you're going to be violent about it—"

"Apparently violence is the only thing that will stop you and your Manual from (as you say) 'taking down the English language.' I don't want it taken down. I want it standing up. The violence you dislike only matches your violations—violations of good sense, good practice, good devices long in use for making reading pleasant. What is the reason for exterminating hyphens like cockroaches? You and your kind managed years ago to prohibit the diaëresis, which was so useful in writing and printing *coöperation, aërial,* and similar words. It made them immediately different from *cooperage* and *aesthetic* and ensured the right pronunciation. And you're the same people who want to reform spelling so that English will be easier to learn! I notice, by the way, that after adopting the form *esthetic*, to which I have no objection, you and your kind have moved back to *aesthetic.* . . ."

"That's because Webster—"

"Confound all those anonymous dictators! Does nobody stop and think instead of reaching for a handbook? If you want to streamline, stick to *esthetic* and *anesthesia* without the *a*—or are you planning a return to *oeconomy* and *oecology*? The cause of this restlessness and handbookishness is that the modern mind wallows in pedantry. It finds its only pleasure in exhibiting the small "fact" recorded in a book by a scribe who worships consistency."

"But you wouldn't have printers, writers, editors go all over the lot, putting down whatever appealed to them at the moment and often not even seeing what they were doing."

"Certainly not! You've described what I think *you* are doing. Your rules change every couple of years—'whatever appeals to you at the moment;' and when you apply them you go all over the lot, blind to your depredations in a piece of writing which, for all you are able to tell, has been carefully considered."

Years ago, Lewis Mumford had to combat his editor's consistency about capitalizing certain words whenever they occurred. He argued that his variations were intentional, for emphasis or the reverse, and sometimes for distinctions of meaning, which he demonstrated. He had his way. The man was obviously 'subjective,' as his would-be improver said. The editor, the firm, the house style, the telephone operator, the chairman of the board were all, of course, objective. Thinking of themselves as packagers rather than publishers, they wanted to "take down" and rub out the individuality of a mind. They really believed, like my interlocutor, that the firm's readers (the author's don't exist) would compare several of their books and exclaim, "My, what inconsistent capitalization!"

"The Rain in Spain," Etcetera

For the last twelvemonth* the literate public of England
has been seething about an issue—or the semblance of one—
which is commonly referred to by the symbols U. and non-U.
Articles, letters to the press, poems derisive and deprecatory,
as well as the unbroken buzz of private talk, have been the
manifestations of this rather uncivil civil war, which we Americans have heard of only through fitful echoes. This is a comforting proof that world communication is not the perfect,
instantaneous thing that orators would have us credit. But our
time is up. The bliss of ignorance is shattered. A publisher
has seen to it, and a book is at our elbow. It is *Noblesse Oblige*,
by Nancy Mitford, with illustrations by Osbert Lancaster—
altogether 160 pages.†

It is a light thing in tone as well as weight, and Mr. Lancaster's drawings suit it well, so that it affords by turns entertainment and a certain sociological interest of a mildly revolting kind. The prose portion is only in part by Nancy Mitford.
She started the controversy, to be sure, but somebody else had
laid the ground for it and many came treading after, a few
angels among them. *Noblesse Oblige* consists of a pair of
essays, a long letter by Evelyn Waugh (the best thing in the
book), an apt poem by John Betjeman, excellent articles by
"Strix" and Christopher Sykes, and a lively introduction by
Russell Lynes giving the history of the battle of words.

*That is, in 1965–66. (Ed.)
†The work was reissued in paperback by Atheneum, New York,
1986. (Ed.)

It all started with a learned article by Professor Alan C. S. Ross of the University of Birmingham, which he published unobtrusively in a Finnish philological review. His thesis was that the only absolute marks of class remaining in English society are words. The upper class uses certain words and no others for many ordinary acts and objects; the middle and lower classes use another, bourgeois, set. The former are U, the latter non-U. "Rich" is U, "wealthy" is non-U; "scent" is U, "perfume" is non-U; "writing paper" is U; "note-paper" is non-U. Further examples and the shorthand in which they are couched are what makes Professor Ross's article scientific.

But this contribution to the science of life would probably have edified no more than a Baltic circle of readers, and thus have been lost to its natural though unscientific audience, if some months after its publication Miss Nancy Mitford had not used the Ross theorem and its symbols in an article eulogizing the British aristocracy. (She calls it the *English* aristocracy, thereby undoing centuries of union with Scotland, Ireland, and Wales, but in this she is consistent with her principles, which are narrow.)

The aristocracy of England, says Miss Mitford, is probably decadent but it is the only genuine one left. Its modes of being, fortunately, are shared by the upper middle class. This is inevitable, since the younger sons and all the daughters of lords are commoners despite their courtesy title—remember Lord *Peter* Wimsey. And Lady Peter too, according to the best English non-sexual logic. Well, this upper crust is sharply distinguished from the stew beneath, and to prove the point, barely two pages from her opening salvo, Miss Mitford pulls in Professor Ross's philology.

She then returns to portraying her class (she herself became a "Hon." by the accident of death, as Mr. Evelyn Waugh affectionately reminds her), and we are treated to a mixture of statistics and psychology intended to convince those whom the thought of a lord does not enchant. She discusses money, love, ancestry, work, and play, and invites us to see the English aristocrat as she does, namely, as the loveliest form of life extant.

But loveliest this time does not mean lovable, except in a rather masochistic sense. For what Miss Mitford admires in her idols is not solely their distinctive manners and proprietary diction, but also their healthy disregard of others and happy instinct for taking advantage of them. In token of which she invents a pleasant fiction about Lord Fortinbras and his family. The best way to show off the aristocrat is obviously to have him encounter his antithesis, the American:

"Comes the war. They [the Fortinbrases] clear the decks by sending Nanny and the children to an American couple, the Karamazovs, whom they once met at St. Moritz and who have sent them Christmas cards ever since. . . . [Later] the Karamazovs, whose lives for several years have been made purgatory by Dominick, Caroline, and Nanny, especially Nanny, send in a modest bill for the schooling of the young people which Fortinbras has no intention of settling. It would seem unreasonable to pay for one's children to be taught to murder the English language. . . ."

So we are back at language. The first thought that occurs to the student of words is that Fortinbras needs a double s to make the etymology clear. A second is that the whole U-and-non-U dispute has a meaning of which the scrimmagers do not seem to be aware. Why should so much heat and seriousness have been generated by a couple of amusing pieces to which their authors obviously attached no importance? The merely fooling intent in both the Professor and the Honorable is shown by the carelessness of each. Professor Ross is sure that in the use of U-terms U-speakers "never make mistakes." Yet he also believes that U-diction changes with the years—*Eh-U fugaces*, as Horace said: non-U terms are promoted U and vice versa; which means that some U-speakers are continually making what others would call "mistakes," simply by changing the conventions of their speech. Professor Ross himself, a U-speaker, writes in a style noticeably academic and non-U, repeating such words as "demarcate" with what is surely no gentleman's relish, and allowing himself the triple solecism of writing: "My son, A. W. P. Ross, kindly calls my attention to, etc. . . ."

Similarly Miss Mitford (who lives the literary life of Paris rather than the lordly life of Horseback Hall) was inspired less by historical or satirical observation than by a mood of aristocattiness against the Americans. She knows them well: "Americans relate all effort, all work, and all of life itself to the dollar. Their talk is of nothing but dollars." The English aristocrat is free of this mania for dollars. He "can augment his fortune in many a curious manner, since he is impervious to a sense of shame. . . . The lowest peasant of the Danube would stick at letting strangers into his house for 2s.6d., but our dukes, marquesses, earls, viscounts, and barons not only do this almost incredible thing, they glory in it . . . and compete as to who among them can draw the greatest crowds. It is the first topic of conversation in noble circles today. . . ."

All this innocent incoherence can be set to the account of lightminded entertainment, but its very existence and that of the rejoinders and supplements by other distinguished authors draw our attention to the hidden point of England's late frenzy. Why such an uproar? And again, why did two very different writers suddenly come together on the issue of language and class? One answer to both questions emerges from reflection on this little book, but it is not a simple answer. One can say that democracy has at last overtaken England and that the "class indicators," as Professor Ross gracefully calls them, are being codified before they vanish. But this is only a part of the reality. There is also a passionate unrest about language and about status being felt throughout the world and it can take strange forms. Scots and Cypriots and men of Goa want "separateness," the Irish would speak Erse, and Zanzibar yearns to be a law unto itself.

The effect of modern egalitarian industrial life is indeed to make men more alike. People buy ready-made clothes, food, ideas. The newspaper and television drum into their heads a common vocabulary. But the result is not cozy; it gives little protection to the ego and little rest to the twin emotions of envy and contempt. Out of the repressed lust for distinction all sorts of petty provincialisms spring up—those of the nationalist, the expert, the sophisticate, the adolescent, the blue blood—emotionally all are one. Part of the original spell of Marxism was its lingo, just as part of the lure and pride of the modern professions is their jargon. Even magazines feel the need of a separate style and go to work revamping the language.

In the face of this vanity of specialism, this multitude of affected and barbarous idioms, one may well regret the passing of a broader, loftier, and finer class speech. But the manner of regretting it is in our authors characteristically modern. Theirs is the love of distinction *against*, without intelligence or principle. As Mr. Waugh informs us, there are indubitably well-born families in which the vocal noise NLU is employed to characterize things and people: Not Like Us. Such a use of abbreviation, including Professor Ross's ungainly pair, is itself a vulgarity; and one that is especially anti-aristocratic when it serves hostile ends. For the ideal at least of aristocratic manners was that of ease, of equality, of sociability. The self kept out of sight and there was no "problem of communication."

Few times and places saw this ideal realized, but when education and large numbers overtook Western society the very virtues of class speech were bound to bring about its corruption. Elegance bred the imitation called genteelism, and *amour propre* fostered a mindless snobbery in both imitators and imitated.

Genteelism is rooted in false shame. In England, for example, the waiter hands you what he calls a serviette and what you (if you are U) must call a table napkin. The waiter's shame apparently comes from the fear that "napkin" will suggest diapers ("nappies") or "sanitary napkin"; and this fear must also affect the upper class, since they take care to prefix the word "table." Only the Americans in this instance show directness and simplicity, the true-blue-U quality.

In most other deviations from high English usage Americans are, as we know, condemned or excused for invincible ignorance. This is but one form of what I have called mindless snobbery. For instance, Miss Mitford inveighs against various kinds of "unspeakable usage" in naming people, particularly that of writing the first and last names in the salutation of letters: "Dear Nancy Mitford." When it was pointed out to her that Henry James used this sometimes convenient form (e.g. to address well-known colleagues who are not acquaintances), she replied: "James was an American."

In general, the English have a very imperfect notion of what an Americanism is. It suffices that the term should be strange to them. Their remarks would accordingly gain in cogency if they leafed through the impressive *Dictionary of Americanisms on Historical Principles* by Dr. Mitford M. Mathews. It is based on the previous four-volume work by Professor Craigie and Dr. Mathews, as well as on an immense amount of fresh research. Hereafter one must consult Mathews before assigning an American origin to some outlandish term. For the surprising conclusion to be drawn from the compilers' labors is that Americans have borrowed, from English and other languages, much more than they have invented. We have preserved, it seems, we are the great conservatives—which is not without its irony in relation to the advocates of Tradition who find us raw.

Again, it is an interesting fact not mentioned by reprovers of American customs that in English aristocratic circles toward the end of the eighteenth century the use of first names was general. By 1820 it had completely disappeared; wives again called their husbands by their last names, as did lifelong friends. The motives behind such changes deserve attention, more so than ever before, perhaps, for the problem of manners is the problem of modern society par excellence. Only manners, good manners conducive to ease among equals, to sociability, can make endurable the moral pressure of so many fellow human beings as we have to deal with.

What then is the genesis of manners? A thing is done either because it has a meaning or because others are doing it. If the others are raucous and inept, the meaning vanishes, leaving only the association of vulgarity. An effort is thereupon made to purify style by abandoning the old usage, and a new cycle begins. From this it can be deduced that snobbery is civilizing or stupid depending on whether it aims at achieving a new grace, at mastering a significant form, or merely at making one-self pass muster with those jealous of their own pretensions.

The English of today, if we can judge by the parties to the dispute (always excepting Mr. Waugh), seem to have no other philosophy but that of futile snobbery. Whether upper or middle class, they stick to a list of Do's and Don'ts. The two lists differ, but each group thinks it is being proper altogether, even though, as Mr. Waugh points out in a classic paragraph:

"Few well-bred people are aware, still less observant, of more than a small fraction of this code. Most people have a handful of taboos, acquired quite at random. Usually at an impressionable age someone has delivered a judgment which has taken root. The lack of reason in these dooms makes them the more memorable, and no subsequent experience mitigates their authority."

And he cites the example of a friend who with deep seriousness declared: "My father told me that no gentleman ever wore a brown suit."

The same irrationality underlies Professor Ross's complacent observation that "a dislike of certain comparatively modern inventions, such as the telephone, the cinema, and the wireless, are still perhaps marks of the upper class." Miss Mitford follows by declaring her reluctance to use air mail, and she virtually guarantees that letters in which she is not addressed as she thinks right are "in silence quickly torn up, by me." Some unhappy beings, one concludes, need the satisfaction of erecting their most trivial prejudices into rules for mankind.

What is regrettable is that the notion of fitness, of utility, of meaning, in short, should be absent from these violent reflexes and censorious emotions. I hasten to add that the contrary American habit, though more amiable, is not more intelligent. Aristocratic speech (*pace* Miss Mitford) is still to be heard in the United States, but the speaker often goes out of his way to search for some vulgar idiom. People fight shy of discussing manners, and among literate or even literary people questions of usage are virtually taboo. This does not mean that we do not feel strongly about language and behavior, but that we are afraid of being thought snobs: we have so much in mind the awful example of our cousins overseas, not to say the memory of their deportment on our doorstep! And so from opposite causes and inclinations, it remains true for us as for them that, in the words of Menander two thousand years ago, "Evil communications corrupt good manners."

"Words Apt and Gracious"

What If—? English *versus* German and French

I am asked what I think would have happened if our national language were German instead of English. My first impulse is to retort: "Why, *isn't* it German?" I think of the thick layers of abstract jargon we carry on top of our heads, of the incessant urge to rename everything in roundabout phrases (Personal Armor System = the new army helmet), of the piling up of modifiers before the noun (easy-to-store safety folding ironing board), of the evil passion for agglutinating half-baked ideas into single terms (*surprizathon* = advertising goods by lottery) and I can only grudgingly concede: "True, it isn't German, but some of it is more German than English."

Had the Pilger Fathers brought with them the pure Plattdeutsch of their time, all might have been well. After separation from its source and under stress of the hard frontier life, the language would have melted and clarified like butter, lost its twisted shapes and hard corners, and become a model of lucidity and force. What only the greatest German writers— Goethe, Schopenhauer, Nietzsche, and a few others—managed to do by main strength in their prose would have been done anonymously by everybody in Massachusetts and in the wagons crossing the plains. Tough characters like Thoreau, Lincoln, Mark Twain, and Ambrose Bierce would not have tolerated the stacking of clause within clause of yard-long words, uncaring whether meaning comes out at the other end. They were articulate beings and they articulated their thoughts —as we are doing less and less every day.

For on our former, flexible and clear Anglo-Latin-French, which we call American English, the überwältigend academic fog has descended and we grope about, our minds damp and moving in circles. Similar forms of the blight have struck the other languages of Western civilization, with the inevitable result of a growing inability to think sharp and straight about anything—whence half our "prahblems."

Had the good forthright people who built this country in the last century met this verbal miasma on landing here, they would have either perished soon from suffocation or made tracks for the open air of Canada, which would now number 210 million. Make no mistake: syntax can change the course of history.

English has a great advantage over German, on the one hand, French and the rest of the Romance languages, on the other, in that it possesses two vocabularies, nearly parallel, which carry the respective suggestions of abstract and concrete, formal and vernacular. A writer can say *concede* or *give in*; *assume* or *take up*; *deliver* or *hand over*; *insert* or *put in*; *retreat* or *fall back*; a shop in New York can even call itself "Motherhood Maternity." The two series of terms are not complete, and the connotations of a word in either set must be heeded before it can be used as a substitute for its first cousin, but the existence of the quasi duplicate makes for a wide range of coloring in style and nuances in thought. Only a mechanical mind believes that the so-called Anglo-Saxon derivatives should always be preferred, and only the starched and stilted will persistently fall into the Latinate.

In contrast, the corresponding words in German always show their concrete origins: *Empfindung* means *perception*, but whereas the English word conceals the Latin *take* (capere), the German keeps in plain sight the *find* (come upon). Similarly, *Gelegenheit* (occasion) has *lie* in it; *abrichten* (adjust) has *straight*; *Verhältnis* (proportion) has *hold*; *Entwurf* (project) has *throw*, and so on. All the everyday words reappear in the compounds. Not merely the associations of these words but their uses and contexts are influenced by this "open plumbing": the abstract idea has not been fully abstracted away.

French, having lost much of its brisk medieval vocabulary during the Latinizing vogue of the Renaissance, has been left with very formal-sounding words for everyday use—for example *comestible* and *consommation* for cases in which we would say *food* and *drink*. The reason why American and English tourists think that French hotel porters are highly educated is that they say such things as: Monsieur est *matinal*; vous allez au *spectacle*; il serait *prudent* de prendre un *imperméable*; c'est un *indigène*; oui, la *représentation* est *intégrale*—and so on. The truth is, no other words are available (except slang), and all these "learned" terms are the familiar ones, just as the highfalutin *emergency* in English is the only way to refer to a very commonplace event.

The results of these contrasting developments in the leading languages of the West go beyond differences of style; they may plausibly be held responsible for tendencies of thought. Thus, when philosophy stopped being written in Latin, the English school that arose was the Empiricist—thinkers who believed in the primacy of *things*: ideas were viewed as coming from objects in the world concretely felt. In French philosophy, *notions* came first: abstract words breed generalities at once, and the realm of thought is then seen as cut off from the world of things, the mind from the body. See M. Descartes. The historians Tocqueville and Taine thought that some of the greatest errors of the French Revolution were due to unconscious and misplaced abstraction.

By the same token, the French language has a reputation—wholly undeserved—for being the most logical of all. For three hundred years French writers have repeated this myth in good faith, because the act of fitting together abstract, generalizing terms lends a geometrical aspect to the product. But French grammar and usage and spelling are full of illogicalities—like those of other languages.

As for German, its lumpy compounds and awkward syntax present a paradox. There is a sense in which a formal German sentence delivers its core meaning three times over—once in the root of the verb, again in the noun, and finally in the adjectives or adverbs almost always tacked on to those other terms. One might therefore have expected that German thought would be peculiarly down-to-earth; yet everybody knows that it has been peculiarly cloudy. The probable explanation is that the words that have to be used for abstract ideas (like *Vorstellung* —"put before") acquire the abstract quality while keeping visible their original concreteness. This double aspect makes the user confident that he is on solid ground. The upshot is the German academic prose that made Kierkegaard, Nietzsche, and William James tear their hair (*Eigeneshaarsichauszupflückenplage*). If anybody is inclined to belittle English for its mongrel character and its "illogicalities," let him remember the limitations of its rivals. We are lucky to have, in James's words, a language "with all the modern improvements."

A Search For Roots

As a man grows older it is likely that the new books to which he forms a permanent attachment are reference books. An encyclopedic reader such as Shaw observed this in himself and on this point, I know, my friends Auden and Trilling report the same experience as I. Hand over to one of us a new Dictionary, "Companion," or Guide, and our eyes first light up and then turn dreamy: we have seized the volume and are off, arm in arm with the guide or companion; the addictionary weakness prevails: we have dropped out of the conversation and fallen into the deep trance of following alphabetized definitions, row on row, the army of unalterable law.

This is not so crabbed and fossilized as it sounds. It does not mean that one is incapable of enthusiasm for a new novel or book of poems. What it means is that it has taken forty or fifty years to pursue and possess the great works of world literature, to discover the no less great works that by accident or perversity only a few recognize, and to pick out from the confetti of one's own times the few precious pieces that define not so much one's mind or taste as one's direction. What more is one offered? In spite of all generous illusions to the contrary, it is not true that a masterpiece in every genre is published every seven days. Only a weekly reviewer believes that, and even he believes it only on the seventh day. From which it follows that in privileged lives, free from reviewer's cramp, the intensity of response to new fiction, new poetry, new philosophies, new criticism, and new histories cannot help being tempered with the years. In compensation, the judgment grows stronger, buttressed as it is by the great piles of octavos incorporated into one's fabric. To have a library of 25,000 volumes under one's belt is a sobering cargo, even if most of them are mere bulk. The eye of the seasoned reader, without being lackluster, is generally hooded, and the mind, if it could be seen, would betray as regards the last sweet published thing a daunting serenity.

Why then does it glow youthfully again at sight of a new reference book? There are two reasons: good reference books are rare, great reference books very rare; and the substance of the good and great in this kind is far denser and richer than that of most other books. To a mind already stocked with ideas, impressions, and systems, the matter of a work of reference gives both an accrual of ballast and a pair of wings. For the contents of such a book are solid and true, yet their variety and arrangement incite to a cosmic freedom. The very letters designating each volume of an encyclopedia are an invitation to dream accurately, to thread associated notions and compel them to form a meaning: "MARY to MUS" says volume 15 of the *Britannica* which I see across the room; what can it be made to tell me without even opening it? Mary, the Virgin, the Queen of Scots, the daughter of Henry VIII; and then the odd notion the French have of calling a double boiler a *bain-marie*: from the sublime (or at least the mighty) to the ridiculous—the ridiculous *mus* or mouse of Horace's *Poetics*, born of the mountains' travail to make a critical point. And beyond it a smaller thing than the mouse, the imaginary *musculus* or little mouse, which by its appearance of running under the skin gives its name to *muscle*, with its mixed connotations of strength, of (musclebound) stupidity, and of criminal (muscling in) violence—the whole a joy-ride on three detached syllables.

Well before the end, the great miracle of language has struck one afresh: its fluidity and power; its progress by error and invention, awkward tongues, bad ears, and punning minds; its untraceable meanders and profound rationality; its idiom-

atic traps producing laughter; and its fitness for making in-
explicable beauty. All this sweeps over one like a flood and
one knows suddenly that one does not want (at least right
now) to think the arid thoughts of fictional beings in predic-
aments standardized by plausibility or momentarily refreshed
by implausibility. One wants, rather, to draw on the wide
memory of vicarious lives and dormant thoughts by following
evocative words to their sources—any words, the words of a
dictionary.

I will not linger to explain how bad an "approved" dictionary can be for the purpose, if one also has literary sensibil-
ities. I only state as a generality that bad reference books on
any subject are marked by spottiness and mechanical judgment, and I pass on to the pleasant task of showing by an
example how the virtues of a great work in the genre give
knowledge and delight without exhausting itself or the reader.

Some months ago* Mr. Eric Partridge, the author of many
books on language, completed and published in London the
work that had engaged his mind for a great stretch of time, his
long-awaited *Origins*. For years, at Christmas, he used to send
his correspondents a thick folded card on which was hand-
somely printed an English word, its ascendants and descen-
dants, with terse comments and illustrations of usage. The
word, it may be said in passing, was never a sentimental re-
minder of the season. "Yule" was left to the headline writers,
who write what everybody reads and no man speaks. Mr.
Partridge had a more humane intention. He was putting together for our benefit his second lexicon, an Etymological
Dictionary of Modern English. This, with his well-known
Dictionary of Slang, is sure to turn the name Partridge into
a superior common noun, like Webster, Fowler, and Johnson.
As we now say: "In a fit of pique he threw the Webster at his
little brother," so our posterity will be saying: "I flew to Cali-
fornia with my Partridge on my knee."

The work is indeed indispensable to anyone who reads and

*That is, in 1957 (Ed.)

writes habitually, and even to those who simply like to know
a little more about the connections of the words they use than
is picked up from casual dealings with prose. I know that
among the demagogues of modern stylistics it is fashionable to
decry etymology. Unless you are an expert, they are quite sure,
you will only be led astray by a little learning of origins. Con-
centrate on reproducing the usages you hear and never mind
the roots. You will be truer to your mother tongue if you play
the game of follow-my-leader in all questions of taste. The
living language, as they never tire of saying, is the unconsidered
speech of Tom, Dick, and Harry. In this game, the leader is
your neighbor and you are his.

But it is equally true that if you want to murder this in-
dulgent mother tongue and permanently muddle yourself and
your hearer, the shortest way is to reproduce without choice
or judgment the usages you hear. Follow the broadcasters and
newspapermen and you will be doing your bit for confusion
by saying *mitigate against* and *forbid from*, using *flaunt* for
flout and *fortuitous* for *fortunate*, and comforting yourself
with the idea that only the depraved palate bothers to distinguish between *masterly* and *masterful*, *momently* and *momentarily*.

Well, no one can or wants to control your lips and tongue,
much less your mind, and Mr. Partridge's book will not of
itself tell you what to say or which words to prefer. Fowler
was there, doing it before him. But suppose one impulse
toward the light of clear reason, one little desire to deviate
into sense, and Partridge can supply it with wisdom while
giving its host enjoyment. For the author of "Partridge" has
studied and grouped the principal words of the language that
belong together through meaning, and he has traced their links
and roots. These interrelations you might, if unaided, guess
correctly, wrongly, or not at all. The chief law of their being is
unexpectedness, which makes reading about them an adven-
ture in a wild garden. Thanks to his brilliant scheme of etymological clusters, Mr. Partridge was able to treat some

10,000 words in the short compass of 950 quarto pages. Take one of these, page 336, as an example of this admirable and illuminative compression: we start with *languid, languish, etc.* and learn that the group comes from the Latin *languere*, which means to be or feel faint. From this we go to *laches, lax, relax, laxative*, and through Old French *relaissier* to *release, lease*, and *laisser faire*, then to *relish* and *leash*, to *delay* and *relay*, to *lash, lack, slack, lag* and *laggard*, to *slake* and *slag*.

On each of these we are given from one to ten lines showing the many languages traversed by the many forms of the one word; we are told how, for example, "*Lack* and *lag* together bring us to the adj *slack*, whence the n and v *slack* with extn *slacken*, and the abstract n *slackness* and the loose, informal trousers known as *slacks*. *Slack*, loose (physically, mentally, morally), ME *slak*, is OE *slaec*, akin to OS *slak*, OHG *schlack*, *slah*, ON *slakr*, a group akin to ON *lakr*, deficient, MD *lac*, deficiency. MIr *lacc*, feeble, (as in para 14)—cf also Gr *lagaros*, slack (of animal's flanks) hollow, s *lagar-*, r *lag-*."

To be sure, it takes a little familiarity with the abbreviations to read this travelogue with fluency. But the very stumbles add to the pleasure, for they may take us to Eg (Egypt), or Port(ugal), and not always north to those damp root cellars ON (Old Norse) and OHG (Old High German). Rarely, thanks to the lexicographer's tireless hunt, are we met by the emphatic symbol of negation: o.o.o., which means "of obscure origin." On the contrary, if we consider that the passage from fanciful and impressionistic etymology to the present high probability of truth has occupied little more than a century and a half, the modern scholar's capacity to follow a clear path around a wide circuit and, as it were, corral a multitude of words and ideas, is astonishingly great. Since the beginnings in the Romantic period, the noting of origins has of course been vigilant and close (*not* "meticulous"; see below). Thus for the avatars of a proper name like Tammany, we have all the needful facts and need not resort to o.o.o. "Tammany, corruption in municipal government, derives from *Tammany*

Hall (orig. occupied by the *Tammany* Benevolent Society) occupied by a political club controlling the Democratic Party of New York City: from the wise and friendly chieftain *Tamanen* or *Tamanend* usu *Tammany*, lit. 'the affable,' who flourished c. 1700." From which we see also that the founding members of the club made a fitting choice among the many available Indian names: "the affable"—what could be better to denote the handshaking politician?

It is less gratifying (*gratus,* received with favor, akin to Sanskrit *gurtas,* pleasing, dear), it is, I say, less gratifying to learn that the albatross, beloved of Coleridge, Baudelaire, and us moderns who do not know what else to hang about our necks, has acquired his poetic name by a series of mistakes. Indifferently a pelican or frigate bird or cormorant, and with his resonant *b* restored to a *c,* he is nothing more than the Portuguese *alcatraz,* which (alas) means "bucket." The Arabic, Hebrew, Phoenician, and Greek roots alike boil down to *kad,* water jar, or as Mr. Partridge tersely concludes: "Basic idea—water carrier."

I have so far suggested two of the uses of *Origins*—as the starting point of an unending tour through the jungle of ideas and objects that man has named, and as an organizer of related sounds and senses. It has a third important use, as a discreet but firm counselor in the choice of written and spoken words. To any one who notices how the strong influence of the visual in modern life has adversely affected common speech, making it often a succession of vague images and ill-concealed metaphors, the search for origins becomes a recurrent duty. Intellectual honesty as well as the old-fashioned art of rhetoric both require that the dead figures buried in the most ordinary words be brought momentarily to life in order to see whether the linking of one image or abstraction with another is proper.

The common absurdity of saying, for instance, "a period of crisis" is more manifest if we know that *period* means a circular road, a rounded, completed portion of time or of discourse; and that *crisis,* which originally means sifting or judging, means by extension the decisive moment in an uncertain course of action, disease, or the like. To regard our century as an age made up of such turning points is ridiculously to flatter ourselves, and at the same time to hide an unlovely outcropping of self-pity. For what the phrase "an age of crisis" really states is our sense of being miserable, more miserable (as we think) than any other age. If this is what we believe, let us say so and stand up for comparison and criticism. Meanwhile, down with muddled Greek; it only puts us in a class with the conceited technician of these days, artist or scientist, who continually coins pompous names for his work by assembling learned syllables misunderstood. *Origins*, I am glad to say, knows nothing of "automation," much less of Jean Tinguely's "meta-matic sculptures." More generally, the book omits scientific terms whose exact definition, if any, can be found elsewhere, and whose derivation is in any case no better than it should be.

But censoring the ridiculous in our speech by a larger awareness of root meanings has a positive side. When that awareness becomes habitual and semi-conscious it enhances the pleasure one takes in any good sentence. Someone wrote of Flaubert: "He was forced to listen there [at his country house] to much conversation that was not simply bourgeois and philistine, but was made still more narrow by provincialism. Traces of this aggravation are abundant in [*Bouvard*] etc." Now that the word *aggravation* has come to mean annoyance, there is pleasure in having the original sense of "worsening," "made heavier" strictly observed in the example just quoted. But to enjoy this doubling it must be perceived, and this takes practice. The writer who fairly steadily uses etymology to amplify or reinforce his intention is composing with chords instead of simple notes, and the listening ear needs training to receive more than the bare melody.

Here we find the reason for the purist's conclusive argument in his running debate with the partisan of market-place usage: the purist, provided he does not abdicate *his* judgment by turning fanatical, can always squeeze more meaning out of his and others' vocabulary than the ignorant or the heedless. It is in him a natural and praiseworthy selfishness to want to retain the full meaning of the richest words. He wants his money's worth of meaning, both to savor it and to make himself understood. If through the usual pedantry of the half-educated, "meticulous" comes to be used as a synonym for "careful," then the additional idea of "fear" in the carefulness is soon lost, and we have two words—one needlessly long and learned—for one commonplace idea. Uneconomic and suddenly ugly, *meticulous* becomes the plaything of the pretentious. What does *Origins* tell us about the meticulose, so that we may see whether the point is indeed lost or still recapturable? ". . . from metus, fear: o.o.o. but the root met- recalls that of L *metiri*, to measure, extn of IE me-: excessive measuring of, hence excessive thought about, a situation. . . ." Therefore, *not* "a meticulous scientist"—measuring is his proper business—but "my meticulous tailor," who measures me to excess for fear that I have impudently departed from his previous norms.

Though *Origins* will draw you in and lead you on in this manner through a mere 10,000 words, do not suppose you will soon come to the end of its stores. In the very nature of words and thought there lies a principle of infinite renewal. Aspects, relations, differences change while you think; you cannot remember them all with finality, for your mind takes you along the one line, however jagged, of your present purpose or dream. Not ten days ago I was reading the meaty article *Fail* and I recall the association *False*. But just now my eye catches again the beckoning sign: *Faucet*, see *Fail*. How do *fail* and *false* generate *faucet*? Did I skip or am I blind? A mystery—but I can always turn the page and follow the lexical imperative, which is: See . . .

A Real Personal Person

Of all the vogue words of the day, *personal* is perhaps the most recurrent. It is certainly the most unnecessary, the emptiest sound in the language. Consider this collection, which anyone can duplicate from the public prints:

She runs a personal bookshop in the country
The artist has contributed a personal and expressive text
The Personal Apartment: Rooms With a Viewpoint
I got a personal handwritten note
According to her personal physician
His personal income is very large
My own personal record at billiards is
We'll send a truck for your personal furniture and carpets
It coiled itself round the tentacles of his personal disappointments
Pure Personal Ivory Soap—4 for 79 cents
Soon everybody will have their personal technology
On Friday he called his personal accountant
Tastefully arranged as a personal dining room
He was found lying in his personal office
My most personal affairs
On a personal note, I will be traveling extensively
You mean you still don't have a personal banker?
I'll be doing my personal best
They pointed out the personal value of his getting the job
Together they write a column on personal health
Each kept a personal diary
Flanked by his personal bodyguard

The woman with whom he had a private, personal rela-
tionship
To write a personal biography, one must
By phone or mail or personal visit to the bureau
A repetition of her personal sufferings
He added those volumes to his personal library
She could only get an interview with his personal secretary
Please look around your seating area and take your personal
belongings
As I have met you personally

What is the reason for this automatic adjective, this obses-
sional trick? I find in it something pathetic; the word seems
thrown in to combat a sense of anonymity, to offset the feeling
that one is being dehumanized and "processed" by life: I want
a *personal* life, in which my *personal* physician belongs to me,
so I can see to it that he treats me as ME, and not just as a
case. And even my apartment had better be personal, or I
shall be tempted to suicide.

The same emotion inspires the highest compliment in
twentieth-century use: "She's a real person"—there are so
many facsimiles, made of plastic and Revlon, that you can live
and couple with and never love or get to know—"as a person."

But this explanation, deep as it goes, does not tell the whole
story or fit all the instances. Behind *personal*, there is also the
vulgar fear of the word *private*, which sounds so wealthy and
undemocratic. The fact remains that since in common sense
every individual is a person and any life is personal to the
bearer, we cannot avoid using *private* when we mean that part
of our person or our life which is sheltered from public view
and concern—business, citizenship, professional work. It is
our *private* life that we enjoy, our *private* diary, unpublished,
that holds secrets about our *private* affairs.

The doctor—alas!—and the dining room, and most of the
others on the list are simply *ours*. They are "personal"—they

are linked with our person—by that simple fact: my library is not the public library, obviously; my visit to the bureau is necessarily in my own person; one cannot visit by proxy; and if my bodyguard isn't personal, what is he protecting? I regret to add that I do own what the brochure says is a Personal Electronic Typewriter, but I would have bought an impersonal one if it had been available. Should I want to add that it is not borrowed from the office, I can say that it is my *private* machine.

There *is* a sense of *person*, and of phrases based on it, which is clear and valuable and ought not to be obscured by the orgy of false uses. "Do you carry much money on your person?" "She felt a light touch on her person." "It was a personal attack" (i.e. not a general one) "You shouldn't make personal remarks" (comments about face, figure, or character). Two more uses are also established but unfortunately ambiguous: *personal appearance* means good grooming or the lack of it, and it has also come to mean *turning up in person*. This second meaning grew out of the early advertising of the film industry when it wanted to say that Douglas Fairbanks was expected to appear at the Paramount Theater in his bodily, three-dimensional form, and not merely on the screen. It is of him on that prime occasion that one might have said "He's a real person."

The abuse now being made of *person* has doubtless been encouraged by two other modern practices. First, the commercial offer to *personalize* an article by affixing to it the buyer's initials. That too carries a sad note, since any set of initials is endlessly duplicated—the same lettered hairbrush must be found on dozens of bureaus, and only the owner and his intimates know what person A.B.C. refers to.

The second influence has come from those who believe that by changing words social prejudices can be removed. Writers are urged to eliminate *chairman, fireman, layman, watchman,* and similar designations and substitute *person* wherever *man* is found. Some publishers and magazine editors, schools and colleges, corporations and government offices, have adopted this policy. It is based on a cluster of misunderstandings and has had a minimal effect on women's salaries and working conditions.

In any case, *person* is not an attractive word, either in etymology or traditional usage. To the Romans, *persona* meant an actor's mask, whether or not the word was derived from *per* and *sonum* (sounding through). I know there is a school of thought that tells us we all play roles at all times and are thus a succession of masks. But if this notion is right, then *person* is not calculated to enhance our sense of identity.

Besides, throughout English history and literature, *person*, *the young person*, and *other persons* have always connoted distance and dislike, if not contempt. "There is a person at the door" does not warm the heart to hospitality. "He found some young person and married her" gives the speaker's judgment with terse finality. In his *Family Shakespeare*, Thomas Bowdler used *person* to replace *body* throughout. In all uses, *person* clearly blots out man and woman, girl and boy. The latest style book of the London *Economist*, the best written of modern weeklies, says: "write *people*, not *persons*," and the statement makes its own case to the ear of the true democrat.

In French, *personne*, though feminine, can be applied to either sex and without disparagement. But it has also acquired the curious meaning of *nobody*. "Qui est là? *Personne*." (Note the French film, *Femmes de Personne*.) The idea of a mask, an empty form until a live being animates it, remains very strong—which rather takes the joy out of being "a real person." Even as an oxymoron—"a real nobody"—it would be a phrase to deplore.

Nor does it shine when compounded: a *chairperson* is an awkward entity to address from the floor. The suffix would be ludicrous with *fire* or *post*; it is impossible in *Minute Man*, *service man*, *gas man*, *clergyman*. It will not work in *man-*

handle or *man* a boat. And one is at a loss what to do with wo*man*. For that -*man* ending is the same there as in the words now being outlawed. Originally *waef-man* or "wife-man," *woman* leads us to the truth about *man*, a truth that the reformers do not know or wish to ignore, namely, that the word has two equal meanings, of which "male" is only one. The other (and earlier) is "human being." As the English Bible has it: "God created man, male and female."

The whole set of related terms and meanings in the western languages go to prove how harmless and neutral the word *man* is—in *mankind, woman, chairman* and their kindred. The Sanskrit root is *manu* = human being; in Latin, its counterpart is *homo*, which later shrank to *on* in French, the impersonal sexless word for *anybody, everybody*. Its analogue in German is *man* (from the other root), while human being is *Mensch*. In English *man* was also, and for centuries, used as a kind of impersonal *on*. Indeed, it is surprising how long it took to settle the gender and use of words relating to human beings: *girl* was at first of the common gender; when Chaucer writes *younge girles* he means young people generally. Others of his time use *knave girle* to refer to a boy, *knave* (German *Knabe*) having no disparaging sense. *Mayden* itself could apply to a male youth, for *maid* meant an adult of either sex. And there was a pronoun of common gender and number, which we still encounter in Shakespeare's *quoth'a*, the unstressed *a* standing for *he, she, it, they* indifferently or together: "See how *a* frowns."

Being derived from *homo*, "human" and "humanity" should therefore be damned and suppressed if *mankind* is forbidden. Yet many patient copy editors cross out this evil word, substitute *humanity*, and feel virtuous—not noticing that their *vir*tue is masculine, not to say *virile*.

Isn't it time this nonsense stopped? Don't personalize: put on initials. All persons are real; it's not enough to mention it and think it praise; but some are loyal, interesting, lovable:

say what you feel. The chairman, fireman, postman have always been with us; give them their due as human beings. And don't forget *Woman*, who as Goethe said, ever draws us upward and has better things to do than haggle over suffixes and sex.

For Us Readers' Sake

All right—NATO and the UN, OPEC, SALT I and II, CBS and NBC, TV, the FBI and the CIA, the IRS and the fifty states and District of Columbia, the G.O.P., LPs and CDs, the Y.M.C.A. and M.I.T., the academic degrees, S.O.S., M.P., and R.S.V.P., plus half a dozen more related to one's hobby or profession, and that's the lot: here ends the list, or should end. Anything beyond is an unwarranted assault on the powers of memory and association, a civil wrong against the willing, attentive reader. The offense is quadrupled if, too lazy to spell out, the author of a book or article makes up a new alphabetic puzzle as he goes along, for the amusement or the illusory convenience of the reader. Now that the classics are being reduced to short-order form for all parties, let me tell you the sad story of the young prince, as nearly as I can remember it.

There was a king at Elsinore, *Hamlet,* or H_1 for convenience. He died so suddenly that some thought he had been murdered, and by his successor at that—Claudius, C, who promptly married H_1's widow Gertrude, G_1. Sure enough, a ghost, G_2, appeared outside the city walls, so the guard called young Hamlet, H_2, who met there his best friend Horatio, H_3. They saw G_2 together, so that the question was: Does $G_2 = H_1$?

Now the new royal pair had a chief minister, Polonius, P, (a symbolic name with a Latin ending, *pole onius,* meaning *stick-in-the-mud*) and he had two children—Ophelia, O and Laertes, L. Between O and H_2 there was at first a love relation (H_2O), and the young men were friendly enough. But C and G_1, and P as well, grew afraid of H_2, who was acting suspicious of all three. To settle these doubts, P hid in G_1's bedroom, behind a curtain that has become famous as the *arras*, or drape with violence, for H_2 stabbed through it and killed old P for his pains.

The rash act did not further H_2O and it got L more than a little upset. Meantime there was a troupe at the nearby RKO or PX, I forget which, with a well-known pair of actors, Incubus and Hecuba, but what she was to him or he to her is not known. H_2 hired them to play a murder scene before C and G_1, but that docudrama did not please. From then on, things get almost too complicated to tell. H_2 is sent off to be killed in a far countree, but he outwits the killers. He returns for the funeral of O, who had died mad at H_2, and to talk with two other friends, gravediggers by trade, G_3 and G_4. He also talks a great deal to himself, and winds up in a row with L.

The end comes pretty fast. At a fencing tournament, everybody foils everybody else with poisoned tips and cups, and the various letters of the alphabet fall in a heap. One that hasn't been used up to that time, F for Fortinbras, a Pole too, but sledding on the ice, comes in and says he thought highly of H_2, as did H_3 and the people. But modern critics disagree; they call his behavior indecisive and cowardly; they dislike his grumbling about the Danish and the drinking. For my part, I think he deserves credit for his single-handed survival tactics against heavy odds. The title of the piece? Well, it's hard to say, when you spell it out in full, whether it means H_1 or H_2—shows how useful numbers are.

For practical purposes in our cluttered organizational life, when we want to refer to institutions, causes, businesses, and political groups, it is always possible to do without initials or acronyms. The mistake is to think that full designations have to be endlessly repeated. In fact, if it is desired to keep the reader awake to what one is talking about, it is much better not to use them. Mention at the start, in full, of course, the *board of directors* or any other division of, say, *the Rockefeller Foundation.* Thereafter, it is enough—it is clearer—to say: the Board, the directors, the Foundation, a Rockefeller program, the executive committee, the chairman, the new planning agency, and so on. There is no need whatever to inflict on the glazing eyeball the RF, the RFBD, the BDEG, and all the other permutations of meaningless letters that now make many a serious page of print look like the components of scrabble.

A further gain is that one avoids such ridiculous vocables as MOMA for the Museum of Modern Art and the revolting irony of AIDS for a dread disease.

It is evident that if initials and acronyms are a blight, and at the same time do *not* fulfill their purpose of making reading easy and rapid, the more recent addiction to the slash or virgule (/) is a similar offense. The earlier use of *and/or* in prose other than legal seemed to have abated somewhat, when the slash returned to spare the slovenly writer the necessity of thinking. We now find a *hero/athlete*, a *tomato/cucumber sandwich, a bed/breakfast option,* a *Baptist/Presbyterian husband/wife* (God will chastise one of this heretic pair!) The affectation has gone so high that the Brooklyn Museum has published an article in its newsletter under the heading: "Working in Brooklyn/Sculpture" and Basic Books has given a work of scholarship the title *Bloomsbury/Freud.*

The first damnable thing about these oblique markings is that they are ambiguous. Whereas a *tomato/cucumber sandwich* may be presumed to contain both ingredients, a *bed/breakfast option* may be taken, for an instant at least, as a choice between eating and sleeping. In other words, you will find the slash equivalent to *and* and to *or*. It follows as a second vice that symbol displaces word, running prose turns into catalogue listing: "Stock No. 361/MR." Thirdly, the symbol means nothing at first, because it is intended to mean too much at the end. "Working at Brooklyn/Sculpture" has to be puzzled out to yield: "working at the *Brooklyn Museum* in the *Department of Sculpture.*" Similarly "Bloomsbury/Freud" must be interpreted as "*disciples and translators of* Freud *in* Bloomsbury."

Granted that these decodings are too long as titles, the slash is not the way to shorten them. *Freudians in Bloomsbury* would do very well. "In Charge of Sculpture" is equally brisk and it is sufficient: in the Museum Newsletter there is no need to harp on *Brooklyn*. Captions even better than these could, I am sure, be found; all they require is a little thought. The presence of the slash is a sign of its absence, that is to say, of the unwillingness to sort out, relate rightly, articulate ideas. In the *Baptist/Presbyterian* couple we cannot be sure who is which, and the noble phrase "husband and wife" is degraded to the level of machinery—the washer-dryer and the reaper-binder.

To conclude: the slash has only one benign use in prose, namely to separate quoted sentences when they occur together in a string, whether enclosed in quotation marks or not. (See the examples on pages 71, 90, and 156.)

The sudden rage to use the slash brings up the cognate subject of hyphens. As an earlier page made clear, the animus of copy editors, abetted by the *Chicago Manual of Style*, makes a dead set at hyphens, supposedly on principle, actually by whim. The principle alleged is that a pair of words designating one thing and in very frequent use should merge into a single word—*screwdriver, overcoat, underline, lifebelt, searchlight, handbook, doorbell*, and the like. The principle will not work. Nobody but John Dos Passos in a weak moment could think that *picturegallery* could ever become a single word. Nor can we readily envisage *coffeebreak, trafficlight, accountbook, seatbelt, wirehanger*, and *those* likes. Yet they are common enough and parallel to the accepted compounds. We write *housekeeper* and *lighthouse*, but would balk at *lighthousekeeper* in one word. Can it be that a saturation point has been reached and we yearn to see our familiar friends separately?

Here a subsidiary principle may raise its head and say: "Of course, some pairs of words don't flow well into a unit and those are excluded." Not true: one sees in print *antifeminist, pseudorevolutionary*, and all the *co-o* and *non-o* words which have become the misleading *coos* and *nonos*: I have spoken elsewhere about the regrettable demise of the diaëresis. The only benefit that came of suppressing it was the useful creation of the word *zoo*. No other seems in prospect. Look again at *anti* and *pseudo*; they are frequent and ever harder to read: *antiinflationary, pseudoauthoritative*—what sane excuse is there for such conundrums?

And how inconsistent are the dictators of the new taste! They decided some years ago that *quasi* should become a separate word, as it had rarely been before. The decision was excellent. Why not then make *anti* and *pseudo* similarly independent qualifiers? "Ah, but *pro*, the opposite of *anti*, is always tacked on." True, but it already forms part of words that existed long before English adopted them as *project, progress, promote*, and it is rarely called on to form new compounds. The reluctance to write *progovernment, proimmigration, propunishment* is the very emotion that shoud apply to *anti, pseudo, non*, and *co*, and sometimes to *semi* (*semiexceptional*). It is common sense: nobody wants to encounter *prog, proim*, and *prop* instead of *pro-* something.

And there you have your true principle: do not print misleading syllables, do not add to those that we are already cursed with. Let there be no mis-leading at the beginning of words and no bad conjunctions within. (This would exclude *firsthand, courthouse, boathook*—all accidental *th*s, and *dish*es likewise—*dishonor, dishonest, dishabituate*; (some people think *dishabille* is pronounced *dish*—). The rule of no bad lumps inside already prohibits *carvingknife, taxshelter, bankbalance*, frequent as these terms are in speech and writing. And the merit of many on the accepted list rather fades when one draws parallels: why a *houseboat* and not a *houseguest, shortbread* and not *shortorder*? Which is the more frequent? Consistency in an*tihy*phening is in fact imaginary.

And what is the matter with hyphens anyway? Do fine printers object to anything that is not a beautiful letter? They seem to swallow without gagging semicolons, question marks, and quotation marks—and the hyphen is so small, the very emblem of the smithereen! While they hunt down hyphens, copy editors should at least remove the one they regularly overlook in "from 1980–85," where it is illiterate to let it stand for *to*, by false analogy with "the period 1980–85."

But one should be ashamed to argue or apologize for the hyphen where it is needed. Readers are not here for fine printers but fine printers for readers. And printers not so fine are now slashing their way virgulously all over the page, so hyphens have every right to perform their old duty.

I would even load a new one on them. I believe in making the act of reading so continuous and fluent that I want to see hyphens wherever two words that belong together in sense are split by the end of the line:

> We then poured a thick gravy, very hot, over her leg of lamb.

> He gave his secretary a book note to type.

> The psychiatrist did his best to put an end to her father fixation.

> No one took notice of the midnight fire alarm.

Once again, the argument that *leg of lamb* and *fire alarm* are not "normally" linked by a hyphen is irrelevant: it is the situation that commands. One might as well argue that *the* is not normally capitalized and therefore must not have a capital *T* at the beginning of a sentence. The point is that a capital at the right place helps one to understand what is going on. So would a hyphen make for more pleasant reading if it were there to impel us forward to the true sense when the end of the line creates a false one.

Mencken's America Speaking

To the nineteen-twenties H. L. Mencken was a dangerous iconoclast, the relentless and often ribald derider of what he called the *booboisie*; a man who consorted nightly with the works of Nietzsche and spent the day tracking down Americana for the inside pages of his "anti-American" *Mercury*. To the forties he began to appear in a second guise—as a voluminous lexicographer; and this, as everyone knows from Dr. Johnson's definition, is to be "a maker of dictionaries, a harmless drudge."

The reason for the change was the publication of his latest work, Supplement One to his celebrated *American Language*. The contrast in reputations was piquant but not convincing. The Mercurial Mencken of the twenties was not a ghoul, and the Monumental Mencken of the forties was anything but harmless. They were indeed the same man, his vocation unchanged. Nor is this a mere impression, but an observation verifiable by dates and facts.

The first edition of *The American Language* was written during the original World War and appeared in 1919. The work grew fat on its maker's feeding and changed internally through four revisions, the last of which appeared in 1945. Beyond revision, it had to be supplemented; but the spirit that animates the whole is the same throughout—a spirit I should like to call, in spite of paradox, satirical love of country. For America was always Mr. Mencken's subject; he fondles it with ridicule; but on a true view both emerge greater from an embrace that often resembles a pugilistic clinch.

Perhaps we have forgotten that the very phrase "American Language" wore in its earlier days an air of defiance and paradox which some found provincial and even chauvinistic. For the name American Language embodied an unfamiliar thesis, which was that the people of the United States had developed their share of English speech into a separate idiom following a destiny of its own. No longer were Americanisms the misdeeds of abandoned colonials; they were the spontaneous and legitimate forms of expression of a people as independent in thought as in polity.

Some time after that first blast, Mr. Mencken went even further and showed that the important branch of the once common tongue was now American and not English. American was spoken by a far greater population and exerted a steady pressure upon English, with hardly any corresponding influence in return. Europe and Asia were learning our words and our pronunciation, and the potential world language, under whatever name it might be adopted, was the American Language.

To point out these truths implied no misplaced patriotism but only philosophical reflection on a mounting pile of linguistic facts. The very nature of American speech, with its great borrowings from Indian and European tongues, its archaisms and neologies, its rapid rate of change and astonishing uniformity over wide areas, made it more than a national achievement: not yet an international tongue, it was already a cosmopolitan medium of exchange.

All this Mr. Mencken was not alone in asserting, though the bulk of professional drudging and dredging followed rather than preceded his initial effort. But what made the four editions of *The American Language*, like his first Supplement, so accessible and hence so influential, was its enormous literary skill and vigilant cultural criticism. As such it stands high in the tradition of the great amateurs, from Dr. Johnson himself to Horne Tooke and Noah Webster.

This is not to say that Mr. Mencken is not also scholarly. He is admirably and delightfully so. His footnotes are as good as his text, and one finds in him that whimsical excess of information which shows a man superior to his system and amused at the ramifications of inquiry. For instance, in explaining the term "baloney dollar," he tells us not only its inventor and its meaning, but also its value and the date of the decree establishing its gold contents. If you want to know the scope of the word *nylon*, you have only to turn to page 341 and learn about the DuPont Company's nurturing of "a whole group of synthetic polyamides." As for a brief history of osteopathy . . . , but the truly marvelous thing is that all these facts, which could be as heavy as lead, and as gray, float and sparkle on a vast Mississippi of comment that sweeps us along and puts everything in its place.

And these waters, though deep, are tonic. For the satirical cast of Mencken's thought leads him constantly to exemplify the qualities of the language he describes. We find twice over, so to speak, the vigor, freshness, and exuberance of the American imagination. Clear, colloquial, astringent, Mencken's prose—like Mark Twain's—reveals its subject and conceals its art. The only ornament it tolerates is a figure of rhetoric which deserves to be called a Menckenism—something that ranges between irony and sarcasm, less premeditated than the first and more impassive than the second, but so sparing of effect that it almost always takes the reader unaware. It is easy, for instance, to take "wilds" literally in the following sentence, but you mustn't, or you will miss the raillery about "Captain Basil Hall, who ventured into the American wilds in 1827 and 1828 and published an account of his sufferings on his return home."

Let me quote again—though in disregarding the author's spacing, one spoils the effect of his shots. Here a trailing phrase shows how soberly Mencken loves his country, even when accusing himself of partiality: "I permitted myself in a newspaper article a chauvinistic sniff, for it was impossible for me to imagine a British don getting to really close grips with the wayward speech of this great Republic." Again, though the American vernacular is his domain, he has a deft way with foreign, technical, or learned words: "Poe, whose *Tamerlane and Other Poems* had come out *pianissimo* in 1827." / "Plans are now afloat to reset the work at the conclusion of World War II and its *sequelae*." At other times, the image involves a social judgment: "The Commonwealth Fund withdrew its support, Lamont turned to forms of uplift less loathsome, and the hundred immortals were never actually appointed." (That is, no academy shall fix our language.)

But do not infer that Mr. Mencken will fraternize freely with the "assiduous members of Rotary and other clubs of organized lovey-dovey." He is not, like "Stuart Chase, busy with the salvation of humanity on a dozen fronts," nor will he democratically accept the "jargon that Dogberries in and out of office use for their revelations to the multitude." Yet he pays a sardonic attention to the complaints of Realtors, a title which "in its early days was frequently assumed without authority . . . [though] a series of legal battles that began in 1925 and ended triumphantly in 1936 disposed of this effrontery." For his journalistic confreres, Mencken has the affectionate contempt that comes of fellow slavery, and he lights it up with a verbal *trouvaille* too good to miss. "The commissioner's studio was abandoned to the *ecdysiasts* [stripteasers], their press-agent, and forty head of reporters and photographers."

The effect of Mencken's sallies against our culture can therefore be compared to the workings of a thermostat: it chills hot air, turns the heat on the philistines, and with an even temper achieves an even temperature. But admirable as it is, this device of blowing hot and cold is often less than adequate to the reader's needs as a user of language, and this leaves one either bewildered or in the clutch of common superstitions. Such neglect involves a threat to the language itself, and something more must be said about it.

Mr. Mencken defends the American vernacular and at the same time is ever ready to laugh at the follies of its makers. Are the fools, then, building better than they know? Or is there a standard by which we can pick and choose among the inventions of a verbally exuberant people? Most of the time, Mr. Mencken thinks there is not. Rather, he grows harsh or toplofty when he has to record the objections of living writers to certain new words. He denounces, with the support of learned philologists, the "vicious purism" that would prune or destroy, and he indulges a retrospective scorn for the eighteenth century, notably for Swift, Gray, and Johnson, who fought against innovations, some of them now part of our speech.

All this confirms the popular superstition I spoke of, which is that by the continual addition of new words language "grows," that the more it grows the more "living" and hence the better it is, and that usage being the only test of life among words, no one has a right to prejudge its verdict. Hands off, therefore, when a new term appears. Intervention is pedantry. For example, Swift at the beginning of the eighteenth century made war on the word *mob*—a slang shortening of the high-brow *mobile vulgus*. Today *mob* is a perfectly respectable word. Inference: Swift was a stuffed wig. More generally: to reprove any modern Americanism is nearly as bad as infanticide, and absolutely like tilting at a windmill.

What is wrong with these notions? In the first place, usage is not the simple thing it seems. Its effect is not only to establish words but also to change their qualities. With the passage of years, *mob* has become disinfected, renovated; it has killed off possible rivals, buried its sordid origins, and acquired proper connections. It is strictly not the same word that Swift disliked—as we can see when we compare it with another short form, say, *rep* (for *reputation*), which Swift also condemned and which is just as tawdry now as then.

In the second place, it is not only the right but the duty of any author in any century to choose his words: that is what writing consists in, and Mr. Mencken's admirable diction proves that he knows this and acts on it. Why then shouldn't writers—Swift or Shaw or Mencken—go one step further and give us from time to time reasons for their choice among the verbal novelties of their day? I say reasons, for in spite of popular belief it is possible to reason out matters of language. It is also important, because words point to ideas and suggest feelings, which together constitute "style" in the sense of moral and intellectual fitness.

Few things are better worth discussing. If the American Language is something to be proud of, the reason is that its words and turns of phrase record fine, great, true, or funny things. This is another way of saying that a language is not a mere device; it is a fund of embodied ideas, the first raw shape of poetry. Hence changes brought about by new forms and sounds in the web of its inner relations are as debatable as a piece of foreign policy or a bronze nude in a public square.

Now for the possibility, so often questioned, of rational argument about language. To appeal to usage, as do the enemies of such reasoning, is to beg the question, for usage is not an agent but a result—the result of innumerable "votes" cast over the years for or against a particular word. The leaders in this popular choice are the men who write and speak professionally—the Roosevelts and Churchills, Hemingways and Audens. If, as often happens, such a man is also a theorist about his own art, he will tell us his loves and hates among vocables. As user and critic, he himself is the voice of usage, himself his own highest authority, with power of life and death over any current form. And as old words are not sacred and may be changed, so new ones are not sacred and may be liquidated. It is the one instance in which rational killing is no murder.

But the word "murder" reminds us that to call a language "living" is a rather slippery notion. Some languages continue to change while others do not or, like unspoken Latin and

Greek, cannot. Actually, what makes a language live is that people speak it, whether or not their newspapermen spawn new expressions every morning. Indeed—and this reinforces the practical importance of arguing about words—it is not hard to imagine a tongue changing so rapidly and breeding so many new terms that it would "die" of overcrowding, confusion, and incoherence. Not every "addition" adds itself: it may displace a clearer, handsomer term, or clutter up speechways until we find ourselves in a jungle barring communication. To put it abstractly, not all growths are equally fit for use, and there is no guarantee that the fittest will survive.

Mr. Mencken admits this in one place, and in a few others shows a willingness to pass judgment on some of the monsters in his studbook. He speaks of words that seem to him "more urban than urbane" and of others whose philistine or ephemeral attributes make them of doubtful value.

Among the latter one finds a product of Chicago journalism according to which a man-hater is called a *misterogynist*. It is not likely that the word will find favor and appear in future classics by satirists yet unborn. But the fact of its coinage—or, rather, its counterfeiting—seems to me the symptom of a disease now attacking American speech. This hybrid word, which takes the Greek root for "woman" and tacks it on to *mister* out of a dim inkling of what *misogynist* means, does indeed betray an interest in words, the interest of pretentious illiteracy.

Daily experience, confirmed by Mr. Mencken's collection, shows that this is no isolated state of mind. When a taxi driver, holding out his palm to the first drops of rain, says: "Another one fraught with precipitation!" or when a soldier, joshing his fellows in slang, winds up with "Aw! don't be unmitigated!" one should perhaps wonder whether spoken American is still the fresh, tough, imaginative vernacular we boast of, or actually past its prime and tricked out in frippery new and stale.

This is the point where I feel that critical lexicographers like Mr. Mencken should give us some principles and rules of thumb. At one time the vagaries of the press or of the downright foolish could be ignored; we could trust to the common language used in more permanent print to keep our speech relatively fixed. But mass reading of mass literature has broken down the dyke. There is no main stream; rather there is a flood of mixed jargons. "Entertainment" and topical books are couched in a slang that will be unintelligible twenty years hence; next to these are their counterparts in academic, pseudo technical, or coterie prose. Pick up for comparison with either sort a mid-Victorian book—say Carlyle's *Frederick the Great*—and you get, not the "stuffiness" that you expect, but genuine colloquial English mixed, like sparkling water, with a little Scotch.

To be sure, there have always been cant words, slang, and academic must; that is precisely the point: they existed and were consciously neglected or attacked. Today we multiply their kind and wallow among them indiscriminately. Only think of the needless enormities we have fashioned and got used to in recent decades: *evaluate* (everything at every turn); *collaborationist; specialistic* (throughout a Harvard Report); *absenteeism* (misused for absences from work); *nourishments* (that is, snacks between meals at military hospitals); *issuance* (usually in *pursuance* of somebody's—not order, but *ordinance*); *radioitis* (and other *-itis* words, quite meaningless); *vis-à-vis* ("be careful *vis-à-vis* the steam table"); *to contact, to implement, to disassemble*—the list stretches on: read Mr. Mencken.

Reliance on the digestive powers of usage alone seems, in these conditions, rather too blithe. It amounts to fatalism, a gay and even perverse fatalism, since its adherents call any attack on these parasitic growths meddlesome and inimical to "life"—as if life in a language were not simply the power to remain intelligible over wide areas and reasonably long periods of time.

Oddly enough, the same Americans who do not hesitate to confuse, misuse, duplicate, and miscegenate words remain humbly conventional in their grammar, especially in print. On second thoughts, there is nothing odd about it, for it is part of the same uncertain desire to show off knowledge, fostered in this case by the etiquette of the handbooks and editorial style sheets. Yet when everybody "knows enough" not to split an infinitive, or makes some similar bugbear equivalent to a knowledge of the mother tongue, it is perhaps time to reconsider what the schools and the books should teach as good English.

In the last edition of *The American Language*, Mr. Mencken had a chaper on "the Future of the Language," part of which dealt with the vernacular as against the "correct" grammar. I am ready to applaud his attack on the conservatism that refuses to sanction well-established popular usages in grammar. Vernacular grammar not only simplifies; its reasoned acceptance would teach us something about the genius of the language that is obscured by our shoddy and excessive word-making. For example, preferring *aint I?* to the prissy *am I not?*; getting rid of *whom*, which is now omitted where it belongs and inserted where it does not; accepting *he dont* (with no apostrophe in this or similar contractions) would really be "modernizing" in a fashion tolerably practical and democratic.

Everyone will at once think of other forms also pressing for recognition—the use of *like* for *as* with verbs, first of all; it is current in the South, in England, in Suburbia; precedents for it exist in the prose of poets from Shakespeare to William Morris and Day Lewis; it is simple, sharp, and clear; and what is perhaps just as important, the enforcement of the "correct" usage has begun to generate absurdities. Last year I read in a dispatch from the front: "As the English, we attacked at dawn."

All these changes would shock—they would shock me, to begin with, but I can see their utility and the desire for it. Of course, they could come to pass only if they emerged as the constant practice of respected writers, eager to remove the bugbears that now preoccupy the minds of those who want to write well and who think they do when they have mastered just these difficulties.

On the same grounds, something should be done about two other stumbling blocks: the right adjective or pronoun to follow *everyone, anyone, nobody, everybody*, and the like; and the use of adverbs with verbs expressing motion or condition: "Pass it quick"—or "quickly"? As to the first difficulty, it seems clear that good sense requires us to say "Everybody took their hats and filed out." *His-or-her* is idiotic. Thackeray, H. G. Wells, Cardinal Newman did not disdain the plural, and it recurs throughout the literary remains of Scott Fitzgerald. If *everybody* aren't plural now, it's high time they were.

As to the second, the right impulse is equally plain: use the short form of the adverb—and do it quick. Swift has "write correct," and the sense supports him. "I feel terribly" should not mean "I am ill (or sorry) but "I am numb," my senses not working. Surely "drive slow," "he talks silly," "don't act insane," are the right vernacular expressions. If the *New Yorker* tidbits bore the caption "This item from Dubuque is reprinted *entire*," we should be spared the awkward "in its entirety", as well as the ghostly presence of "this item, reprinted entirely."

Other concessions to instinctive practice might follow. I think we fuss too much about dangling participles, as the "logical" French do not. Only a few danglers are ludicrous or reprehensible. Let us also have the so-called fused form— "I can't stand him grumbling"; it is not quite the same as "*his* grumbling" and distinctions are worth having. Even so, I should be willing to forget the differences between those erratic duplicates, *lie* and *lay*, though I am not willing to die a martyr to this cause.

To adopt some of these new habits, though some are old enough—"There let him lay," wrote Byron—would naturally seem to many a piece of gratuitous violence. Yet that is how change, "growth," improvement, simplification, and all the kindred merits we vaunt in our speech come about. Their justification is that they are responses to a need felt by many speakers and writers when they are *using* the language, not fiddling with it.

That is the important difference. The coiners whose words I attack respond to needs outside language: the advertiser wants to sell; the journalist wants to astonish; the bureaucrat wants to impress. You may say the writer similarly wants to charm or persuade, but presumably as a craftsman he cherishes language and follows rules arising from his daily handling of it—rules that are often hard to state, but which those other improvised tinkers do not even suspect exist. Neither does the neutral public that endures when it might be made to judge. Hence my regret that Mr. Mencken, the satiric guardian angel of our national soul, should not hold it a part of his great task to exhibit formally, side by side with his own genius, that of our language.

On the Necessity
of a Common Tongue

As one looks at the state of our public and private life, one is struck by a paradox. On the one hand, whatever social and individual freedom we enjoy is a product of pluralism in theory and practice. On the other hand, every move made for the extension of freedom to the so-called minorities results in demands for a self-centered, exclusive separateness which is the opposite of pluralism. A strong desire prevails *not* to engage in "conversation." Groups emphasize their roots; the public schools are beset by difficulties of "communication," in whatever language; and bilingual programs try to offset this return to quasi tribal existence. These programs cover not just the few large groups one readily thinks of as speaking English unwillingly or with difficulty—the Black or Hispanic; the number of languages offered comes to eighty-five and includes many aboriginal tongues as well as dialects. But there is doubt whether the teaching leads to schoolwork in American English; the tendency seems rather to reinforce the existing barriers, to re-create distinct nationalities: not cultural pluralism but cultural solipsism.

This attitude naturally goes beyond the mere use of a vocabulary and grammar. Language molds our thoughts; it gives color and shape to our desires; it limits or extends our sympathies; it gives continuity to our individual self along one line or another. These effects occur whether we are conscious of them or not. It is fair to say that they are not deliberately sought, but the resistance to changing native ways of speech *is* deliberate; it is an effort at self-assertion to preserve something valuable. It also assumes that all languages and dialects are of equal value. That is the tragic mistake, the self-inflicted wound that may be fatal; and tragic and fatal not merely to the nation that suffers this resistance, but to the resisting individual and his legitimate hopes.

The false assumption about language comes from pride, of course, but also from ignorance, both understandable enough. Still, that state of mind and feeling raises the question: Is a standard language necessary? The question deserves to be settled, not arbitrarily by the native speakers of a dialect or of Standard, but reasonably by all those who can be brought to judge the facts of the case. What are these facts? They fall into two sets, whose meanings are not hard to grasp. The first set of facts has to do with the character of a widespread standard language; or, What makes it different from some other kind of language? The second set of facts has to do with the origin of a standard language; or, How did it come to possess that character?

We start with a fact that we all feel instinctively—the difference in the forms of speech that we use on different occasions. Casual talk with an old friend differs from the language used during an interview to obtain a job. These kinds shade into each other, overlap in vocabulary and grammar at many points, but at the extremes the words and the forms—vocabulary and grammar—are noticeably unlike. There are even differences in the speech that one finds natural in different moods: remembering a birthday party or a funeral brings different ranges of words to the mind. All this is to say that language is a flexible instrument which responds to the thoughts and feelings of the user; it adapts itself to the present occasion and the purpose in view.

But the fitness of a word or grammatical form is not determined solely by the user; it is also arrived at by a kind of social decision. The habits of surrounding speakers compel us almost automatically to use what is appropriate. Yet here again differences may occur. At the funeral, for example, some over-sensitive souls will be careful to say "passed on"; the more forthright will say "died"; and only the hostile or heartless would say "kicked the bucket."

It is these variations in response to individual and social choice that cause all the difficulties and arguments implied in the terms: Standard English, substandard, colloquial, slang, dialect, and jargon. If a language were a uniform means of expression; or if its varieties could be clear-cut; or if, again, those varieties were not linked with certain other things that people take as signs of low or high education, of economic status, social habits, and even moral and religious attitudes, the question of language would not arouse such feelings or bring up the great matters of democracy, equal rights, elitism, and snobbery.

That being so, if one truly wants to think about human speech without prejudice or rancor, one must try to suspend judgment until one understands how language does its job. Take, to begin with, the type of language which goes by the name of *cant* or *thieves' argot*. It is a vocabulary based on the standard speech, but so altered that only the thieving fraternity can make out a meaning. By extension, the term *argot* can be applied to special words used by any group, even though they do not intend to conceal their meaning. Shop talk among people of one trade or profession is such an *argot*, largely unintelligible to an outsider; a landlubber finds it hard to follow the conversation of sailors about sailing. But that is a result of his ignorance; it is not the intention of the users. The more usual name of this kind of professional or trade speech is *jargon*.

What may we conclude about these types of speech, which are related to the mother tongue, but which differ from it and from each other while using many of its resources? Just one thing—that they are limited; they do not cover the whole range of experience; and they are exclusive: by confining the users to certain kinds of expression they prevent the non-users from understanding what is being said.

These two results, of exclusion and of limitation, lead to what is really a very obvious idea—the idea that a larger, all-purpose language for everybody is clearly desirable. The need is for a set of words and grammatical forms that every native or adoptive user can be expected to understand and to find adequate: in other words, a standardized language. With such a language one need not belong to a special group, whether of thieves or sailors, mechanics or lawyers, in order to attempt to speak it. It belongs to all trades, professions, all groups, ranks, and even to all peoples if they will only learn it. Its utility is plain: it brings together through a common medium of verbal exchange the largest possible number of people, in one nation or more than one. Such a language is a common currency whose value is known at sight.

It might be supposed that sensible people would recognize the fundamentally democratic character of a standard language—a language designed to be the same for all users regardless of special interests. But because the standard tongue has sometimes been described as the language of the best writers and speakers, because it is the language of the educated and the successful, of the so-called opinion leaders, it is believed to be their property alone, so that in recent years it has been attacked as a device of snobbery and oppression. It is charged with putting at a disadvantage those who do not know it or do not handle it well. And in reaction, the feeling has developed that local, limited forms of speech are better than Standard—better for the group of users as being more natural and also as being their inherited possession, which should not be taken away or altered from outside.

To put this argument in linguistic terms, *dialects* have been ascribed a value superior to that of the standard idiom. This doctrine tries not only to reverse the previous ranking, dialect now claiming superiority; it is also trying to reverse an evolution of the last thousand years of Western civilization. Dialects start as languages limited geographically as well as in range of expression. The name "dialect" implies that grammar, vocabulary, pronunciation, and idiom look and sound distinct from Standard without being so different as to form a separate tongue. It is this betwixt-and-between character that tempts the admirers of dialect to deny the merits of the standard language and attack it as a cruel imposition.

At first sight, the dialect looks as if it could serve all the needs of its users just as well as Standard—and more easily. But it does not. To begin with, it may be unintelligble in the next township. Consider an example from outside the area of debate. England, small as it is, still shows here and there pockets of surviving dialectal speech in the midst of Standard. The contemporary English novelist V. S. Pritchett recalls in his autobiography how, when he was a child, his parents moved from London to Yorkshire, where the other children spoke a dialect hard for him to understand, while his accent and vocabulary made him a virtual foreigner. Yorkshire is about as far from London as Chicago from Peoria; this gives a measure of one of the limitations of dialect.

But there is worse. Dialect falls short in breadth of vocabulary and flexibility of construction and it usually lacks a literature that records past experience; in short, dialect denies access to the full range of ideas and feelings that a civilization has discovered and given names to. Its rigidity is an emotional and intellectual strait-jacket, for a dialect does not produce much—if any—formal writing, and so it does not steadily enlarge its means of expression like the standard tongue.

A standard language keeps up with new discoveries and with new ideas and feelings by means of new words and idioms, which are in turn organized and preserved by the written record. Without the written word, seconded by the art of printing, a widespread language would slide about and, by uncontrolled change, scatter its resources in so many directions that it would fail of its single purpose, which is: ready communication among the largest possible number of fellow speakers. And this large number—let us not forget—includes the users of past generations and those to come. One has only to look at another special language—slang—to see how insufficient it is and how rapidly it perishes. Slang excludes the majority of native users except for the short time when a phrase is in vogue. To repeat, jargon, dialect, slang are exclusive by nature. The standard tongue is the democratic form of the language par excellence.

The issue, therefore, between the standard tongue and any dialect, however attractive in itself, cannot remain one of patronizing regard for dialect on the part of the educated or of "rights" and preferences on the part of minorities. Short of the total population, numbers are irrelevant; for in various circumstances of life every one of us may find himself or herself in a linguistic minority, sometimes a minority of one. It happened to me when as a youth I found myself in England speaking only French. It happened again a little later when, having learned English-English, I came to the United States and heard around me many words and pronunciations I was unfamiliar with. Fortunately, from my early days in London all the way to this very moment, I have been able to stay in touch with other people—thanks to the broad unity of the standard tongue: it is hospitable enough to include London English, American English of the Northeast, the American English of Texas or Ohio, as well as my own mixed kind of speech: none of them excludes a traveling minority such as myself, which a dialect would inevitably do.

To keep up a standard language, then, is simply a practical endeavor. It is especially practical for the members of cultural minorities. For among their rights is surely that of full self-development, which presupposes self-knowledge and self-expression. Development and expression alike depend on the command of a sophisticated and flexible instrument of thought

—and there is no other but the prevailing standard language.

Consider just a few of the daily-life situations in which command of the common tongue is important, the importance ranging from the convenient to the indispensable: travel (avoiding misdirection or being taken advantage of, overcoming the sense of being lost and forlorn); reading (news, warnings, pleasant or profitable opportunities); employment (applying effectively, qualifying for interesting work); love and friendship—the point hardly needs elaboration.

Nor should it have to be said that if a highly gifted child is born in a family and region where a dialect or "local standard" is the first language, the recognition of his or her gifts and their use for the public good through a brilliant individual career depend on that child's early mastery of the wider standard tongue, oral and written. No one is going to reach the bench of the Supreme Court speaking only Cajun or Sicilian. A truly pluralistic society must take care of its human resources regardless of where they come into being, and as the United Negro College Fund says in its appeals: "A mind is a terrible thing to waste."

When one stops to think about these plain, virtually platitudinous truths, it seems incredible that anybody professing a liberal outlook and applying it to the language question should argue for the perpetuation of dialects and speak of Standard as optional. If acted out, such a "philosophy" would mean holding a citizen imprisoned within the confines of his origins. Free and endowed with the common rights in other respects, this person is told by the sentimentalists that he need not open the gate to the common speech. One can only be amazed to discover that professional groups of *teachers of English* have gone on record as favoring school programs that reinforce attachment to native forms of speech and that represent Black English as sufficient to open careers to talent.

The liberal outlook, as a businessman of Hispanic origins has pointed out, dictates the opposite policy. Speaking of the growing practice of translating notices into Spanish, he says: "Fair play? I think not. Unfairness would be to deny these people the opportunity to learn English." And he goes on to speak of opportunity as a general right which includes the opportunity to learn Standard.

These arguments from ordinary life are self-evident, but they are not the only potent ones, they are only the most obvious, as another writer has shown when reporting a fact that would not readily come to mind: Lack of a common language is a barrier to psychiatric help, and it turns out that some Hispanic patients cannot make themselves understood even to a physician who speaks the standard form of their own Spanish dialect. This in turn reminds one that for the same reason school children in certain bilingual classes resist the Spanish or other foreign medium of instruction, because it differs from their own dialect of that same language. Nor with that dialect is it possible to teach them, for it lacks the terms of arithmetic—or whatever—that are required for elementary instruction. As well, in these conditions, make the jump to English—and Standard English at that, with due allowance for transitional stages and, needless to say, avoiding any offense to the feelings of the learners.

Certainly, the position of Standard as the most widely used, most popular of all modes of speech in the nation need imply no disrespect toward dialects or other tongues, any more than formal writing disparages colloquial conversation. As we saw at the beginning, in matters of language, appropriateness to circumstance is the only guide, and the standard tongue is the appropriate device for individual and national life in modern civilization.

At this point someone might object: all you say about the characteristics of Standard is true. Nevertheless, for a good many people in this country, in any country, the prevailing standard speech is alien; it is the language of just another group, which happens to hold power and wants to force this group language on "our" group in an arbitrary exercise of authority.

That view of the situation is plausible but contrary to fact. I do not underestimate the emotions involved. I know at first hand what strong feelings bind one to the tongue of one's birth, how unhappily one gives it up for another. But the objector's reference to group rivalry and hostility is misguided. Standard is the very opposite of a group language, as I tried to show by the example of my own travels through at least three groups which, had they lacked a standard tongue, would be speaking three foreign languages—foreign to each other. Would anybody today maintain that American English is a dialect of original English? No, and why not? Because the differences are slight and the exchanges of new words between them continually keep them in touch. By that means we—all of us— are also kept in touch with one another.

But there is a further sense in which the standard language is not "just a group language," and to show what that sense is brings me to the second set of facts I mentioned at the outset. In earlier times, when travel was difficult, when there were no good roads and no mechanical means of transport (let alone means of communication such as printing and broadcasting), every region spoke either a tongue or a dialect foreign to its near neighbors. In Europe, such a form of speech might be original or derived from some earlier Standard. Thus after the European sway of Latin, the bits and pieces of the Roman Empire fell into dialects.

Out of these dialects, slowly, a few arose as new standard tongues—Italian, French, Spanish, and—with a special admixture—English. The causes of these developments were various, but what often decided which of several related forms became more general was somebody's attempt to use that particular form in literature. Usually it was the form already most popular, or perhaps the one that seemed most flexible and rich. It appealed to a poet (Dante, Chaucer), to a translator (Luther), to a printer (Caxton), or to some other person or persons to whose bold initiative we owe the crystallizing of a modern European language. Their work encouraged imitation, made contacts easier over an ever-widening territory, and spurred all users to continual invention, in keeping with the changing needs that the speakers encountered century after century.

A standard language is thus a creation over time by a whole people, an achievement kept in being by its speakers and in order by its literature. That is why I said it is the very opposite of a dialect. Instead of being narrow and self-contained, the standard tongue draws to itself needed words from neighboring dialects, from related foreign tongues, from the ancient dead languages, from distant places all over the earth. Writers and thinkers make up idioms, phrases, proverbs, clichés, which are circulated by their works—one may regard Shakespeare as a mass of clichés; and the uneducated also contribute wonderful things—short-cuts in grammar and syntax that simplify, or happy transformations of learned words that keep the language plain and vivid.

Standard, then, is everybody's handiwork without distinction of rank or fame. It is moreover an international product, English more so than any other tongue; its vocabulary contains large imports from Latin, Greek, Spanish, French, Portuguese, Dutch, and Italian; and also from Arabic, Malay, Hindu, Chinese, and American Indian. Indeed, when one considers the vast accumulation of words—and of ideas caught in the words—which the *succession* of standard languages has piled up for our use, one sees such a language as English as a great work of art on which all mankind has spent its gifts. For behind every language of Europe, including Latin and Greek, lie the Sanskrit roots first spoken in India; and they, by some path or other, go back to man's very first efforts at articulate speech.

This large legacy from the past is surely very far from a group language in the local or regional sense. But perhaps the

sight of that richness and complexity is what makes it forbidding, even more than its association with literature and the
powerful. After the many masterpieces of prose and poetry
that one finds in every great modern tongue, Standard is un-
questionably difficult to master, and a dialect by comparison
looks cozy and sufficient as well as "natural"—no effort is
needed to speak it and few care to write it. But if one yields
to this feeling, one must accept the restricted life to which
dialect condemns the user. Make this other comparison: would
those who can use the standard tongue, yet advocate the suffi-
ciency of dialect, think the same way about arithmetic? There
are peoples who can count only up to five—would the dialect-
clinger argue that our complex number system is too difficult,
an unnecessary refinement and a cruel imposition?

The good sense of the matter is, of course, that no one need
become a mathematician in order to benefit from the numbers
beyond five and the multiplication table. Similarly, there is no
need to become a Noah Webster to benefit from Standard
English. But every child other than the retarded, as the Coun-
cil for Basic Education has shown, can acquire the fundamen-
tals of numeration—and of standard literacy as well. Every
child is in fact eager and inquisitive about words and numbers
until balked, repelled, and stupefied by bad teaching, or more
often by non-teaching long drawn out.

There is no blinking the fact that if a standard language is
to survive as a means of communication on the widest possible
scale, it must be taught. True, many learn it by trial and error,
"at the mother's knee." But circumstances, especially in the
modern world, may interfere with that seemingly natural beginning. The mother works, or is inattentive, or impatient, or
thinks it wrong or unnecessary to correct infant ways of
speech. Others learn instead the ways of dialect which, as we
saw above, immediately confine the mind and the tongue
within the walls of a region, class, or ethnic group.

Ten or a dozen such enclosures may coexist within a nation
as large and as recently settled as the United States. And there

each dialect is even farther from the other dialects than it is from Standard in the important features of—let me repeat—grammar, vocabulary, idiom, and pronunciation. So it is not a question of all the dialects together waging a successful war against the "imperialism" of Standard—that is a meaningless statement. Isolation from Standard, if it succeeded for any group, would be a cutting off pure and simple from the entire remainder of the population. Think of India without English: its native tongues number over three hundred. In the Philippines (7,000 islands and rocks), twenty-four languages and dialects flourish, and none is dominant, but English is used in the schools and may in time bring unity of speech. It is the persistence of a standard language that provides the series of overlaps by which a dialect speaker and a Standard speaker may, with luck, partly understand each other; two speakers of different dialects hardly ever can.

So we come back to the proposition that in order to maintain a standard tongue it must be formally taught, and taught to everybody for the sake of practicality—general convenience and individual self-development. In the most literal sense, the language which is standard in the nation is everyone's birthright.

Now, one of the reasons why such a language is standard is that it follows certain forms and not others—not the dialect forms, to begin with, and not the many other forms that might exist or that uneducated people fall into, the forms called mistakes because not in good use. Some people think mistakes in English do not exist or do not matter if the speaker can be understood by the hearer. It's not so simple. In one of those places in England where dialects still linger, a boy will say to his girl: "If thee be to me as I be to thee, name the day." Well, that urgent, charming invitation is *in* English, and we all understand it readily. But it is not Standard English, as we can also see without explanation.

Every foreigner learns that fact about hundreds of turns of phrase that sound quite sensible to him and that might indeed have become English, but did not. And every native must learn other, similar facts, if it so happens that he has picked up—or made up—usages that are not recognized as standard by those who pay attention to words.

By tradition it is at school that one learns the adult use of the standard tongue, and one learns it most thoroughly by writing. The connection between writing and a standard language holds from start to finish. That is why courses in English combine writing themes with reading books. The books supply examples of good prose, stretch the vocabulary, and enlarge the student's actual stock of thoughts and feelings by familiarizing the mind with their clear expression. This development of the person through a language that is itself developed cannot be achieved in any other way, and it is a further reason why a standard language is at once justified and necessary.

Knowing the role that literature has played in framing and developing Standard English and holding it in shape, one feels today that the issue of dialect *versus* Standard is intertwined with a second and perhaps greater issue. From all sides one hears that some of our main difficulties come from a "failure of communication"—in government, in business, in the professions, in domestic life itself. Granted that misunderstandings arise from feelings and not solely from words, there is nevertheless a link between the two that should not be overlooked. What is uttered accounts for a great part of the blundering, falsehood, anger, contempt, despair, and violence that are concealed under the euphemism of failed communication. And these bad words or wrong words, spoken or written, reflect the current state of the standard tongue, its tone and quality. Today, neither of these can be called good. Why not? Because of habits and conditions tending toward abuse and disintegration.

These conditions are easily summarized. The language has been overloaded with jargon—the users most highly educated in the arts, sciences, and professions have fashioned virtual dialects which violate the plainness and clarity of Standard and its great literature. One of the motives to this corruption has been the desire to seem special and profound. Picking up the habit, government uses the same language with the different motive of evasion and painless euphemism. Business and advertising share both motives and add to the pseudo technical language the metaphorical, which also blurs the contours of reality. And the common man, brainwashed in this murky medium, comes to use no other. He too is pedantic and metaphorical, which robs his thought of concreteness and coherence.

Surprising as it may sound, I cannot resist the conviction that we owe this quasi universal development not alone to the obvious influence of science and technology, but also to that of the poets and novelists of the last hundred years. It was they who taught us how to reassign meanings to words—not occasionally but steadily—at the same time as they showed for syntax a disregard all too easy to imitate. It would be an exaggeration (but also a convenience) to call the many examples of this distorted tongue "Joyce's Revenge"—Irish against English. But of course the causes go deeper, and some of them I have tried to detail elsewhere.

The standard tongue was only helped to its birth by literature; it will not perish solely by it. Nor is its recovery ruled out. Nothing is fated and English can survive if the users will it so. But to succeed they must remember that just as the common tongue is the birthright of everybody who learns it, so it belongs to the community, not the individual. He has no property rights in it to warrant demolition, only the use of it for one short lifetime. Such great wealth can only be held in trust.

ACKNOWLEDGEMENTS

The chapters in this book that first appeared elsewhere will be found in the following places:

"Preface" ("Why Quibble, Horatio?"), *Columbia*, XI, 1, October 1985

"The Positive Side of Negatives" ("Don't Avoid, Pursue!"), *Writer's Digest*, LXVI, 6, June 1986

"It Makes No Sense," *Columbia*, XI, 5, April 1986

"English As She's Not Taught," *The Atlantic*, December 1953

"Enigma Variations," (as by Roger Du Bearn) *American Scholar*, XXXVI, 3, Summer 1967

"Le Faux Chic," *American Scholar*, L, 4, Autumn 1981

"What Makes Writing Right?," *International Journal of Cardiology*, V, 1984

"Watch For Trouble Ahead," *Columbia*, XI, 2, November 1985

"Promiscuous Pairs" ("Verbal Abuse"), *The New York Times Magazine*, August 17, 1980

"Tonier Than Thou," *Columbia*, XI, 3, December 1985

"Page Mrs. Malaprop," *Columbia*, XI, 4, February 1986

"Vulgar, Vulgarity, Vulgarisms," *Columbia*, XI, 6, June 1986

"Basic English" (" 'The Republic' in Basic"), *The Nation*, April 25, 1942

"Fowler's Generation," *American Scholar*, XXVI, 3, Summer 1957

"The Rain in Spain," *The Griffin*, V, 8, July 1956

"What If? English vs. German and French," *The Phenomenon of Change*, Cooper-Hewitt Museum, New York City, July 1984

"A Search For Roots" ("Not All Are O.O.O."), *The Mid-Century*, No. 12, May 1960

"A Real Personal Person" (expanded from "Vulgar, Vulgarity, Vulgarisms," *Columbia*, XI, 6, June 1986)

"Mencken's America Speaking," *The Atlantic*, January 1946

"On the Necessity of a Common Tongue" ("Life and Language"), *Three Talks by Jacques Barzun*, Northern Kentucky University, Highland Heights, KY, 1980

SELECTED BIBLIOGRAPHY:
OTHER ESSAYS ON LANGUAGE
BY JACQUES BARZUN

Essays on Writing, Editing, and Publishing, 2nd ed. University of Chicago Press, 1986.

"Unhyphenated American," *Nation*, September 5, 1942.

"How to Suffocate the English Language," *Saturday Review*, February 13, 1943.

"A Second Language," *Saturday Review*, October 2, 1943.

"Architects of Babel," *Saturday Review*, July 1, 1944.

"The Counterfeiters," *Atlantic*, May 1946.

"On the State of the Language," *Harper's*, January 1949.

"The People *vs.* Free Speech" (review of Eric Partridge, *English: A Course for Human Beings*), *Nation*, Oct. 15, 1949.

"More on Sound Repetitions," *Word Study*, April 1950.

"The Retort Circumstantial," *American Scholar*, Summer 1951.

"The Greater Garble," *Saturday Review*, April 12, 1952.

"Words and Ways of American English," *New York Herald-Tribune Book Review*, August 3, 1952.

"Not Gobbledygook, But Plain Words" (review of Sir Ernest Gowers, *Plain Words*), *New York Times Magazine*, August 21, 1955.

"A Chance to Tinker to Evans" (review of Bergen Evans, *A Dictionary of American-English Usage*), *American Scholar*, Winter 1957.

"Watch Your Language" (Preface to Theodore Bernstein's book of that title). New York, Channel Press, 1958.

"High Jinks and Pathos—a Review of Eric Partridge's *Dictionary of Slang and Unconventional English*," *Mid-Century*, November 1961.

"What Is a Dictionary?—a Review of Webster's Third New International Dictionary," *American Scholar*, Spring 1963.

"Some Hints About Writing," in *Britannica Book of Usage*. New York, Doubleday, 1980.

"Sherlock Holmes and Sociology" (a letter), *American Scholar*, Spring 1981.

"Rhetoric and Rightness: Some Fallacies in a Science of Language," in *The Creating Word*, ed. Patricia Demers. London, Macmillan, 1986.

"Look It Up, Check It Out," *American Scholar*, Autumn 1986.

INDEX

About the Book

This book was typeset by Heritage Printers of Charlotte, North Carolina, in Linotype Times Roman with Times Roman display type, was printed by letterpress on 60-pound Warren's Olde Style paper by Heritage Printers, and was bound by Arcata Graphics / Kingsport of Kingsport, Tennessee. The endpapers are French Marble, imported from France by Andrews / Nelson / Whitehead of New York City. The design is by Joyce Kachergis Book Design and Production of Bynum, North Carolina.

WESLEYAN UNIVERSITY PRESS, 1986